The Last Days of Jesus

François Bovon

Translated by Kristin Hennessy

Westminster John Knox Press
LOUISVILLE • LONDON

© 2006 Westminster John Knox Press

Originally published as *Les derniers jours de Jésus: Textes et événements*. Deuxième édition revue et augmentée. © Labor et Fides, Genève, 2004. First edition: *Les derniers jours de Jésus: Textes et événements*. Neuchâtel: Delachaux & Niestlé, [1974].

Book design by Sharon Adams
Cover design by Lisa Buckley
Cover art: Crucifixion. © *André Burian/Corbis*

Published by Westminster John Knox Press
Louisville, Kentucky

This book is printed on acid-free paper that meets the American National Standards Institute Z39.48 standard. ⊛

PRINTED IN THE UNITED STATES OF AMERICA

06 07 08 09 10 11 12 13 14 15 — 10 9 8 7 6 5 4 3 2 1

Library of Congress Cataloging-in-Publication Data

Bovon, François.
    [Derniers jours de Jésus. English]
    The last days of Jesus / François Bovon ; translated by Kristin Hennessy.—1st ed.
    p. cm.
    Includes bibliographical references (p.   ) and index.
    Contents: Sources—The methodological starting point—The unfolding of events—Times and places—Conclusion.
    ISBN-13: 978-0-664-23007-4 (alk. paper)
    ISBN-10: 0-664-23007-5
    1. Jesus Christ—Trial. I. Title.

BT440.B6813 2006
232.96'2—dc22   2005058466

Contents

Preface

With both joy and hesitation did I accept the request made to me by Gabriel de Monmollin, the Director of Éditions Labor et Fides (Geneva), to consider and then to prepare a second edition of this slim volume. Before accepting his proposal, I consulted, with the help of Jonathan von Kodar, to whom I extend my deep thanks, the principal works published on the subject since the appearance of the first edition. I noted several very worthy recent studies, whose titles can be found in the bibliography at the close of this volume: to the names mentioned in the first edition's preface I must now add James S. McLaren, John T. Carroll, Joel B. Green, Alan Watson, Peter Egger, Simon Légasse, Raymond E. Brown, Francesco Amarelli, and Francesco Lucrezi. Yet this investigation also enabled me to perceive that few new documents have joined the sources already under study at that earlier time. In fact, the conditions for writing a history of the passion have remained rather the same. The same conditions still trouble the attempt, but they do not prevent it. Faced with this situation, I sought the opinion of Adalberto Giovannini, professor of ancient history at the University of Geneva, to request his judgment of my text. He encouraged me to republish this brief study. He did, however, admit that he was in the course of developing a new conception of Roman penal law, which he intended to apply, in his next book, to the Christianity of the first centuries. When that work appears, my findings here shall have to be compared with those elaborated there. In any case, I am grateful to this friend, who took the trouble to read and comment on this work.

While this study does take a historical perspective on the events of the passion, the religious dimension of its subject cannot be ignored. Throughout the centuries, the polemic between Christians and Jews has been fed by readings of Jesus' passion as recounted in the Gospel narratives.[1] The problem of anti-Semitism in the New Testament has elevated these tensions further. But the ever-contemporary nature of the subject under study here has not tempered my eagerness; rather, it has encouraged me to strive toward an honest and acute inquiry. From the start, then, let us recall that Jesus was a Jew, and that the opposition he awakened, first in Galilee and later in Jerusalem, typified the tensions that arose around the prophets of Israel. Let us also remember that Christian communities, up until the end of the first century CE, constituted a movement internal to Judaism, a new "heresy," to borrow the expression of Flavius Josephus, the Jewish historian of antiquity. Further, I should add that the first Christians, like many Jews of the same period, sought the protection and support of the Romans in opposing the Greeks. It follows that many Christian sources, like the Gospel of Luke, manifestly aim to minimize the responsibility Pilate bore in Jesus' trial and death. Despite this tendency, however, no one dared efface the memory of the crucifixion, a Roman penalty, to substitute instead a punishment in conformity with the prescriptions of Moses' law. This study aims to show that the religious and political grievances the Sanhedrin brought against Jesus were indissoluble at that time and that, for this reason, the Jewish authorities cannot rightly be accused of dishonesty or hypocrisy. We can only hope that an accusation of deicide has disappeared forever from Christian consciousness. I am convinced that human culpability cannot be transferred from generation to generation. It is not fair that children should have damaged teeth because their par-

---

1. The Gospels tend to emphasize the responsibility of the Jewish authorities in Jesus' trial; for an examination of this question, see Simon Légasse, *Le procès de Jésus, l'histoire* (Paris: Cerf, 1994).

ents feasted on sour grapes. Who now would think to condemn twenty-first-century Romans for the assassination of Julius Caesar, any more than the French or English of today should bear the blame for the centuries-old judgment of Joan of Arc? Let the death of Jesus be viewed as it demands, with the limited dimensions of an isolated event, belonging to a vanished past.

What has changed most, perhaps, since the first edition of this book, is this author's own consciousness as a historian. I perceive more clearly today the limitations of any historical inquiry. I understand more fully than before that any description of the past is a reconstruction, that even the most objective examination of testimonies and sources will be imprinted with the identity and concerns of the examiner. In light of this understanding, it is right to avow from the outset that this volume's historian is a believer and, further, a Christian theologian. But it is also right to add that this author refuses to succumb to that which he can only call the defeat of understanding. I continue to believe—in spite of prejudice and what the Anglo-Saxons call the "biases," conscious and unconscious, of the learned—that communication between human beings is possible, and that agreement can be reached from many sides through the interpretation of the same evidence. The practice of history has grown more complicated since the age of Theodor Mommsen, but it has not grown impossible. This, at least, is the presupposition under which the following pages proceed.

While few corrections have been made to the first edition's text,[2] several precisions have been added. I have come to regard the *Gospel of Peter*, for instance, as an important source, though it received little attention in the first edition. I have questioned here the identity and function of the Sanhedrin in ways I previously did not. I have explained in more detail the reasons I deem Jesus' words from the cross to be inauthentic. I would have wished to provide the reader with an appendix of all the texts of

---

2. One important correction concerns the alternation of sources within the Lukan passion narrative. I hold today to the hypothesis that Luke drew for these chapters from two documents, the Gospel of Mark and Lukan special material, rather than to the hypothesis that he drew solely from the Gospel of Mark.

the passion narrative; such voluminous documentation proved overwhelming, however, in the space of this brief work. Instead, I resolved to retain only the canonical Gospel of Luke, to which I have devoted particular study in the form of a commentary published elsewhere, as well as one noncanonical text, the *Gospel of Peter*, evidently less well known. These two texts form an appendix to this work.

All scriptural citations, with a few minor emendations by the author, follow the New Revised Standard Version of the Bible. The excerpt from the Third Gospel found in the appendix also comes from this translation.

With Mikeal Haxby's collaboration, I have brought up to date this volume's bibliography, while maintaining its chronological presentation.

Finally, I would like to express my deep gratitude to Kristin Hennessy, who, building on her superb knowledge of French and her elegant English style, has produced this excellent translation. I enjoyed working with her and discussing the nuances of this translation.

F.B.
Cambridge, Massachusetts
September 2005

Preface to the First Edition

This small volume bears no scientific pretensions. It does not aim to rival the classic monographs of Joseph Blinzer, Paul Winter, or Pierre Benoit. Instead, it responds to a certain popularizing intention. A popular presentation need not, however, preclude a critical approach. The public surely deserves to know the hesitations and conflicts shared by historians and exegetes. Thus this volume does not try to silence controversies where they arise, nor does it neglect to present the conclusions its author has drawn from these controversies. My primary concern here has been a methodological one. Too many works on Jesus' trial, even highly scientific ones, prove remiss on this account. For this reason, the present volume attends primarily to examining the sources it presents, to choosing a legitimate point of departure for its inquiry, and to elucidating a realistic unfolding of the events it reconstructs. While this study belongs to the field of history, that specificity need not signify that its conclusions are without theological import. Recent scholarship has in fact rediscovered the value of inscribing the revelation in history, in its psychological, social, political, and economic contexts. Historical clarifications only contribute to the theologian's project.

The subject treated here, embracing as it does the subtleties of history, exegesis, and law, has demanded that I call upon the collaboration of diverse specialists. I give thanks to two professors of ancient history, Denis van Berchem, from the University of Geneva, and Jean Béranger, from the University of Lausanne, as well as to Pierre Cornioley, professor of Roman law in the Faculté de droit at the University of Geneva. These three scholars have granted this study the benefit of their expertise. I wish also to express my gratitude to Jacques Meylan, a friend and doctor in law, who willingly read the manuscript and offered the fruits of his critical attention. Finally, I thank Daniel Roquefort, who compiled this volume's index. As the reader will see, annotation has been kept to a minimum, in the hopes of not burdening the reading experience. The specialist will quickly discern the many debts to previous work incurred throughout this work, as well as the places in which this work departs from its predecessors. I hope that the bibliography at the close of the volume will compensate for the sparseness of its notes.

F.B.
Begnins, Switzerland
1 August 1973

Introduction

Illumined by the resurrection, Jesus' death originates two movements that have marked Western civilization to this day: Christianity and anti-Semitism. But for the cross at Golgotha, Christian communities would not have come to light; but for the growth of the ancient church, the hatred directed toward the Jews would never have become so violent. In light of these religious and political repercussions, a historical study of Jesus' trial seems necessary.

Christian theologians have paid particular attention to Christ's passion, for it is the origin of their faith. Despite innumerable erudite studies, however, the last light has not been cast on this affair. Numerous and diverse difficulties arise from varied factors: first, our sources require subtle treatment; second, our knowledge of Jewish penal practice and Roman provincial law in the first century CE is fragmentary and unsure; third, the convict, Jesus of Nazareth, remains a mystery in both action and intention; and finally, Christian and Jewish experts who have applied themselves to this study often have lacked objectivity.

This last obstacle proves perhaps the most difficult to surmount. For centuries, in fact, Christians have held a preconceived image of Jesus' trial: condemned for blasphemy by blind Jews, the Son of God, though blameless, was put to death. Such a historical reconstruction bred within the church a hatred of those on whom it pronounced blame. But if Christians have had difficulty

1

abandoning these prejudices in order to analyze historically the death of the one they honor as Lord, Jewish scholars, whether consciously or unconsciously, have often shifted the responsibility for Jesus' death onto the procurator, Pilate.

In the following pages, I will attempt to reconstruct the events that took place in Jerusalem between Palm Sunday and Easter Sunday. I will first present and assess the available sources, noting the evident remove between the events themselves and the first written sources concerning them. I will also take into account the inevitably subjective process of interpretation with which participants in the drama, eyewitnesses, and then members of the church have viewed the historical events. In history, we must remember, bare facts are irretrievable: an event can be viewed only through the mediating language that narrates and, in narrating, interprets it. Any witness will reconstruct, according to a particular understanding of the events, how the events unfolded. Though at first this process yields a variety of interpretations, over time the authority of certain interpreters reduces variety to uniformity. First and foremost, then, the historian encounters the claims made about the events that took place.

Chapter One

Sources

In addition to several Christian, biblical, and noncanonical sources, a few Jewish and pagan accounts also lie at the historian's disposal. The Gospel passion narratives, in their extant form, are broad narratives, reworked by the church. Though the most familiar narratives, the Gospels date from around 70–100 CE and do not in fact provide the most ancient accounts of Jesus' trial and death. In this chapter, I will present successively each source pertinent to this study, beginning with the most ancient.

Pauline Epistles

The apostle Paul, the earliest known Christian author, cites liturgical fragments in his letters. Among these hymns and faith confessions, discovered through New Testament scholarship, we find the most ancient accounts of Jesus' death. Though these texts evoke Jesus' death and resurrection, they do not enter into historical details. Rather, the two events, proclaimed as reality, have gained already a metahistorical dimension in the eyes of Christian faith. Thus does Paul announce in 1 Corinthians 2:7–8: "But we speak God's wisdom, secret and hidden, which God decreed before the ages for our glory. None of the rulers of this age understood this; for if they had, they would not have crucified the Lord of glory." The salvific significance of the two events interested the earliest Christians more than the historical contingencies that caused them. In line with this interest, Romans 3:23–26 presents the cross not primarily as a historical event, but as an event of sacrifice: "All have sinned and fall short of the glory of God; they are now justified by his grace as a gift, through the redemption that is in Christ Jesus, whom God put forward as a sacrifice of atonement by his blood, effective through faith. He did this to show his righteousness, because in his divine forbearance he had passed over the sins previously committed; it was to prove at the present time that he himself is righteous and that he justifies the one who has faith in Jesus." First Corinthians 15:3–5 presents Jesus' death and resurrection as those of the Messiah: "For I handed on to you as of first importance what I in turn had received: that Christ died for our sins in accordance with the scriptures, and that he was buried, and that he was raised on the third day in accordance with the scriptures, and that he appeared to Cephas, then to the twelve." In Philippians 2:5–11, the one who died is shown as a preexistent being entering into history: "Let the same mind be in you that was in Christ Jesus, who, though he was in the form of God, did not regard equality with God as something to be exploited, but emptied himself, taking the form of a slave, being born in human likeness. And being found in human form, he humbled himself and became obedient to the point of death—even death on a cross. Therefore God also highly exalted him and gave him the name that is above every name, so that at the name of Jesus every knee should bend, in heaven and on earth and under the earth, and every tongue should confess that Jesus Christ is Lord, to the glory of God the Father." Finally, in Romans 4:24–25, the events of Good Friday and Easter Sunday are invested with the power to grant forgiveness to the believer: "It will be reckoned to us who believe in him who raised Jesus our Lord from the dead, who was handed over to death for our trespasses and was raised for our justification."

Outside these few phrases, the Pauline and deuteropauline epistles offer little historical information. At the most, 1 Thessalonians 2:15 references the role of the Jews, "who killed both the Lord Jesus and the prophets," 1 Corinthians 11:23 links the institution of the Eucharist to "the night when he was betrayed," and

1 Timothy 6:13 mentions a "good confession" that Jesus made "before Pontius Pilate."

Acts Accounts

The missionary speeches in the Acts of the Apostles are the work of Luke's hand. Though, in their present state, they are redacted compositions, they nonetheless retain traces of more ancient, traditional textual strata.

The majority of the passion accounts in Acts (2:22–24, 36; 3:13–15, 17–18; 4:10–11, 25–28; 5:28, 30; 7:52; 10:39–41; 13:27–29) contrast Jesus' death, a human work, with his resurrection, a divine work. Those to blame for the first event are Jewish leaders and the residents of Jerusalem. Yet, however unhappy their action, it allows for the accomplishment of God's plan. Lines from the Pentecost sermon that Luke attributes to Peter exemplify this view: "You that are Israelites, listen to what I have to say: Jesus the Nazorean, a man attested to you by God with deeds of power, wonders, and signs that God did through him among you, as you yourselves know—this man, handed over according to the definite plan and foreknowledge of God, you crucified and killed by the hands of those outside the law. But God raised him up, having freed him from death, because it was impossible for him to be held in its power" (Acts 2:22–24).

When the Acts accounts do specify the historical unfolding of events around Jesus' passion, they stress the action taken by the Jews in handing Jesus over to Pilate and the trial before the governor. Only one text attributes judgment of Jesus to the Jews themselves: "Because the residents of Jerusalem and their leaders did not recognize him or understand the words of the prophets that are read every sabbath, they fulfilled those words by condemning him. Even though they found no cause for a sentence of death, they asked Pilate to have him killed. When they had carried out everything that was written about him, they took him down from the tree and laid him in a tomb. But God raised him from the dead; and for many days he appeared to those who came up with him from Galilee to Jerusalem, and they are now his witnesses to the people" (Acts 13:27–31).

Leaving aside for a moment the question of Lukan redaction, these texts suggest a traditional schema for preaching to the Jews. This schema comprises two elements: first, the Jews accuse Jesus before Pilate, who commands his execution; second, God resurrects Jesus. Compared with pre-Pauline and Pauline texts, this schema remains more closely linked to the historical unfolding of events.

Now, Lukan redaction tends to harmonize this traditional schema with the passion narratives found in the Gospels. From this harmonization, for instance, come allusions to Barabbas (Acts 3:13–14) and Herod (Acts 4:25–28). One discordance does trouble this harmonization: according to Acts 13:27–29, Jesus' burial was accomplished by hostile Jews, not by Joseph of Arimathea, as the Gospels recount. On the whole, however, the traditional schema—which may well not have recognized any veritable trial before the Sanhedrin—resisted the influence of the larger Gospel narratives.

Passion Predictions

In their current form, the passion predictions of the Gospels (Mark 8:31; 9:31; 10:33–34, and parallels) do not derive directly from Jesus, but from the Christian tradition. Though Jesus certainly sensed his coming death (see Matt. 23:37–39), he could not have described it with the precision of the predictions in Mark. Two traditional phrases preserved in Luke (13:32 and 13:33) suggest Jesus' expectations more accurately than the passion predictions. Though the two phrases do not agree between themselves, they are distinct from the Christian tradition in that they use the schema of the three days to refer to the stages of Jesus' life and especially his ministry, rather than to the time that separated Jesus' death and resurrection, as the passion predictions do. The more archaic of these two expressions has Jesus speak in the following way: "Listen, I am casting out demons and performing cures today and tomorrow, and on the third day I finish my work" (Luke 13:32).[1]

---

1. See François Bovon, *L'Évangile selon saint Luc (9,51–14,35)*, CNT 3b (Geneva: Labor et Fides, 1996), 395.

The passion predictions handed down through Mark's Gospel, especially the third of these, suggest a different, yet still traditional, schema for the passion events. There the passion, described in terms of God's plan ("the Son of God must undergo," Mark 8:31), unfolds in four stages: Christ is first handed over to the Jewish leaders, then to the pagans; third, he is executed; and, finally, he is raised after three days. This fourfold schema seems to provide the traditional structure from which the passion narratives were composed.

Gospel Passion Narratives

Over time, the fourfold schema suggested by the passion predictions was augmented with individual pericopes drawn from independent traditions. Through this accretion, the passion narratives were gradually assembled, piece by piece. In this process, the events confessed in pre-Pauline formulas and the Lukan schema for preaching to the Jews were also included. Most likely, these narrations responded to a liturgical need. Now, evidently not every Christian community followed the same eucharistic liturgy. Certain communities, venerating Jesus only as teacher and prophet, may not have celebrated a eucharistic liturgy at all. But many communities, particularly those in Jerusalem and Antioch, wished to recall within the context of a sacred meal the decisive events that had marked the passion and resurrection of their Lord. They determined that this particular narrative, by virtue of its magnitude and solemnity, suited itself to ceremonial retelling. Thus the passion narrative, in diverse forms, served as both the foundation and motivation for the liturgical rites these communities celebrated. In adopting this usage, the first Christians came to link story and liturgy as the Jews and the Greeks did, retelling their sacred, collective origins within the context of their ritual celebrations. The Christian liturgy thus became the *Sitz im Leben* for the forming Gospel passion narratives. Such liturgical usage, likely an annual occurrence, explains the close resemblance and unity of the four Gospel narratives.

Despite a larger unity, each Gospel passion narrative is marked by distinctive characteristics; let us now turn to the principal characteristics of each. The whole of Mark's Gospel probably was composed with a view to its end point, the passion. Given this overarching orientation, it proves difficult to say where the passion narrative begins, whether at Mark 11, with the entry into Jerusalem, the cleansing of the Temple, and the conspiring of the priests, or at Mark 14:1, with the plot to kill Jesus. At chapter 14, in any case, the focus locks definitely on Jesus' fate: the plot to kill Jesus (Mark 14:1–2); the anointing at Bethany (14:3–9); Judas's betrayal (14:10–11); the preparations for Passover (14:12–16); the designation of the traitor (14:17–21); the Last Supper (14:22–25); the walk to the Mount of Olives, Peter's denial foretold (14:26–31); Gethsemane (14:32–42); the arrest of Jesus (14:43–52); Jesus before the Sanhedrin, mockery (14:53–65); Peter's denial (14:66–72); the second meeting of the Sanhedrin, Jesus before Pilate, Barabbas (15:1–15); the humiliation of Jesus (15:16–20a); the movement toward Golgotha, the crucifixion (15:20b–27); further humiliations (15:28–32); the death of Jesus (15:33–39); the bystanders at the cross (15:40–41); the burial (15:42–47); the empty tomb (16:1–8).[2]

Through this narrative, Mark aims to show readers that Jesus' death is neither an accident nor a fatal conclusion. Instead, the death marks the end of a necessary series of events originating in the divine plan. The crucifixion itself seems to hold a double meaning: first, it signals the close of the battle Jesus has waged with Satan (the Second Gospel progressively escalates the opposition between Christ and Satan); second, it brings about the redemption of humanity by the forgiveness of sins (the Second Gospel presents Jesus' ministry as a service offered on behalf of all humanity).

The Gospel of Matthew closely follows Mark's text, with a few additional developments to the narrative, such as the death of Judas (Matt. 27:3-10), Pilate washing his hands (27:24), the guards

---

2. A majority of the most ancient manuscripts attest that Mark 16:9–20 was not present in the primitive version of this Gospel. These verses were added in the second century CE to compensate for the absence of resurrection appearances in Mark.

at the tomb (27:62-66), the guards' report (28:11–15), the appearance of the Risen One, and the commissioning of the disciples (28:16–20).

From a theological point of view, Matthew emphasizes that Jesus' death, as a fulfillment of Hebrew Bible prophecies, proves his perfect obedience to the demands of the Law. His ultimate submission to God in death is accompanied by his complete refusal of supernatural power. Only by first renouncing any use of power does the Matthean Christ come to receive all power. Thus, in a proleptic fashion, the Matthean Christ legitimately displays the signs of his sovereignty from the very moment of his passion. He also establishes by his death a new covenant, one that offers pardon to the faithful and founds an ecclesial community. In this community, believers answer the divine call and set forth on the way of faithful obedience. Finally, Matthew underlines the eschatological nature of Jesus' death and insists on the continuous presence of the Risen One with his community.

The Lukan narrative differs widely from the one that unfolds in Mark.[3] To begin with, the anointing of Jesus by the woman appears early on, at Luke 7:36–50. The institution of the Eucharist (Luke 22:14–20) precedes the designation of the traitor, inverting Mark's order. In Luke, the Last Supper includes a farewell discourse treating on true greatness, Peter's fate, and the equipping of the faithful (22:24-38). The announcement of Peter's denial, again unlike Mark, here precedes the departure for the Mount of Olives. Given these differences, some scholars have claimed that Luke did not follow Mark, but rather used an independent passion narrative, perhaps related to the tradition used by John. Other scholars contend that the evangelist used Mark exclusively but selectively, subjecting it to vigorous revisions. The most probable explanation seems that Luke, according to his

---

3. See Erika Heusler, *Kapitalprozess im lukanischen Doppelwerk. Die Verfahren gegen Jesus und Paulus in exegetischer und rechtshistorischer Analyse*, NTAbh, NF 38 (Münster: Aschendorff, 2000); Alexandru Neagoe, *The Trial of the Gospel: An Apologetic Reading of Luke's Trial Narratives*, SNTSMS 116 (New York: Cambridge University Press, 2002).

custom, drew from two sources, Mark's narrative and his own Lukan special material, which he then interwove with skill.[4] The two documents were similar enough that he could fit the best parts of each together in an alternating pattern: Luke first follows Mark's narrative for the episodes of plotting and Passover preparations (Luke 22:1–14); then he turns to Lukan special material for the scene of the Last Supper and the farewell discourse (22:15–46); returning to Mark, he takes up the arrest, Peter's denial, the humiliation of Jesus, the appearance before the Sanhedrin, and the trial before Pilate (22:47–23:5). Then, for the Herod episode, the interlude with Barabbas, the condemnation of Jesus, the road to the cross, and the crucifixion, he follows again Lukan special material (23:6–43). For Jesus' death and the scene at the empty tomb, Luke draws anew on Mark (Luke 23:44–24:11). The final episodes of Peter's visit to the empty tomb, the meeting on the road to Emmaus, the resurrection appearance to the Eleven, and the ascension (24:12–53)—all episodes found only in Luke among the Synoptics—surely derive from Lukan special material.

Within this broad narrative plan, many particularities arise in Luke that are pertinent to the subject of this study. The midnight meeting before the Sanhedrin disappears in Luke. Partial contents of this scene (Luke omits, for instance, Jesus' saying on the Temple) are moved to the morning meeting with the Jewish authorities (Luke 22:66–23:1), a meeting elsewhere mentioned only by Mark (Mark 15:1). Only Luke recounts Jesus' appearance before Herod Antipas, tetrarch of Galilee, and the following humiliation (23:6–12). Though Luke does not mention the soldiers' mockeries (see Mark 15:16–20a), he alone relays a conversation between Jesus and the thieves who share his hour of execution (Luke 23:39–43). These singular episodes, as suggested above, derive from Lukan special material. So, too, do the final scenes of the Lukan passion narrative—the disciples at Emmaus (Luke

4. See François Bovon, "The Lucan Story of the Passion of Jesus," in *Studies in Early Christianity* (Tübingen: Mohr Siebeck, 2003), 74–105.

24:13–35), the resurrection appearances at Jerusalem (24:36–43), the final instructions of the Risen One (24:44–49), and the ascension (24:50-53). All drawn from this same source, these episodes appear uniquely in Luke among the Gospels.

For Luke, Jesus' death fits into the divine plan, having been attested to by the prophets. Though he does not emphasize the redemptive significance of the cross, Luke does present the beneficial value of Jesus' death. When Jesus, the righteous one, dies the death of the unrighteous, he opens the way for the reconciliation of sinners. Jesus also dies an exemplary death, teaching his disciples to renounce human power and, in this renunciation, to triumph through the only true power, the Holy Spirit.

Chapters 18–20 of John's Gospel diverge even further from Mark's passion narrative than Luke 22–24 have done. Though the primitive four-stage schema of passion predictions appears also in John, the details of the unfolding events quickly distance John's narrative from the one found in Mark. The plot against Jesus appears as early as John 11:45–54. Next follow the episodes of the anointing at Bethany (12:1–8), the entry into Jerusalem (12:12–19), and the Last Supper (13–17). In John 18:1–11, Jesus is arrested, though he utters no final prayer to his Father here; this prayer falls earlier in John (12:27–28) and bears little resemblance to those of the Synoptic Gospels (Jesus does not ask to be spared the cross). The detachment that performs the arrest, probably including Roman soldiers, takes Jesus to the high priest, Annas, for interrogation (John 18:12–23). Annas then sends the accused before his son-in-law Caiaphas, the high priest serving that year (18:24). John's Gospel does not include a trial of Jesus before the Sanhedrin. The account of Peter's denial falls between Jesus' appearances before the two high priests (18:25-27).[5] The principal scene of John's narrative follows next, with the appearance of Jesus before Pilate (18:28–19:16). In a remark-

---

5. John 18:12–27 poses thorny problems for the exegete. Anton Dauer offers a minutely detailed analysis of its problems in *Die passionsgeschichte im Johannesevangelium. Eine traditionsgeschichtliche und theologische Untersuchung zu Joh. 18, 1–19, 30,* SANT 30 (Munich: Kösel-Verlag, 1972).

able movement, Pilate shuttles back and forth between Jesus, seated in the praetorium, and the Jews, waiting outside for fear of defilement. Here the silent Christ of the Synoptics yields the floor to the loquacious Johannine Christ (witness his responses on the kingdom of God, truth, etc.). If John depicts, with the Synoptics, the Barabbas incident, he alone evokes the *Ecce homo* scene (19:4–5). So too do we find in John's crucifixion scene (19:17–37) circumstances and sayings no other evangelist records: the mother of Jesus and the beloved disciple appear at the foot of the cross (25–27); Jesus pronounces the words "I am thirsty" (28) and "It is finished" (30); and soldiers pierce his side with a lance (31–37). The burial, as in the Synoptic Gospels, comes about through the generosity of Joseph of Arimathea (19:38–42). Finally, after the discovery of the empty tomb (20:1–10), there follow three appearance stories, to Mary Magdalene (20:11–18), to the disciples (20:19–23), and to Thomas and his companions (20:24–29).

Theologically speaking, John shows a more profound early Christian view of Jesus' death than that encountered thus far. All of Jesus' life, in fact, converges in John toward this single "hour" that enacts the elevation and glorification of the Son. Christ's passion, that passage from life to death, becomes above all his return to the Father and the passage from death to resurrection. To this one event—the ultimate achievement of Christ—corresponds the universal scope of the salvation offered, from the cross, to all who believe.[6]

These four passion narratives tell a story, a history. But they are not disinterested accounts by objective witnesses. They are testimonies of faith. Those who composed them, little by little, deemed that Jesus' untimely end fulfilled God's ultimate end, revealed at last in the resurrection. Recently, scholars have striven to distinguish in these narratives between prophecy historicized and historical events narrated in light of Scripture. The former category describes stories invented in order to insert into

---

6. See Martinus C. de Boer, *Johannine Perspectives on the Death of Jesus* (Kampen: Pharos, 1996).

history the providential fulfillment of prophecies. The latter describes remembrances of real events shaped by readings of biblical books. To make so sharp a distinction between these two narrative practices, however, seems inappropriate. A firm division has never existed between invention of the first type of stories and transformation of the second type. Rather, a rich dialectic has always existed between the way events influenced the understanding and selection of biblical texts and the way biblical texts influenced the shape given to remembered events. There has always been interaction between the memory of facts and the recall of texts. In reality, the process cannot even be delimited to these two poles. Other factors, like the contemporaneous situation of communities who felt visited by the Spirit or the experiences of inspired believers, informed the process of remembering and narrating from the very start. Such circumstances influenced the exegesis of scriptural texts, just as they guided the selection of those memories the community would not forget.

Other factors further inflected the passion narratives. Along with the kerygmatic and liturgical influences noted above, there was a decidedly apologetic tendency to the narration of the passion. If this tendency can be felt as early as Mark, it grows progressively in the later Gospels, manifesting itself in two primary strands. The first was directed to the Jews, for whom a man condemned to death and hung on a tree, far from being a potential Messiah, was in fact further condemned by the Law. In response to this view, the evangelists stressed the divine plan attested to by the Scriptures and fulfilled in Jesus. Despite appearances, they insisted, the cross was the intended mystery of God. The evangelists used scriptural witness, drawn above all from the Psalms and Zechariah, to support their paradoxical theology, valorizing a seemingly unjust condemnation and failure. The second apologetic tendency was directed toward pagans, to whom the cross was a disgrace. The evangelists aimed—in accordance with their missionary goals—to exculpate the Romans, particularly the governor, Pontius Pilate. Thus Matthew depicts Pilate washing his hands of the affair, Luke has him pronounce three times the innocence of the accused, and John shows Pilate handing Jesus over to the Jews that they might crucify him.

In addition to this apologetic tendency, two other tendencies must be brought to light, a parenetic or moral aim and an orientation toward the legendary. The parenetic tendency evinced Jesus' courage with a view to encouraging Christians to suffer in following him. To this end, for example, the Gethsemane scene exhorts believers not to follow the dozing disciples, but to remain ever vigilant. The second tendency, a legendary orientation, caused the passion narratives to be amplified by new details, details developed in accordance with the rules then governing popular narration. Under this influence, characters received names, such as Malchus of the severed ear (John 18:10) and Peter, agent of the imprudent swipe (John 18:10–11). Similarly, hitherto unknown events suddenly found their way into the narrative, such as the healing of the wounded ear, which Luke alone recounts (Luke 22:51), and the dream—favorable for Jesus—dreamt by Pilate's wife (Matt. 27:19).

Some scholars hold that the subjective and kerygmatic nature of the Gospels not only inflected the meanings given to narrated events, but actually caused the evangelists to betray historical fact outright in the narrating of events. In light of this view, these scholars have hypothesized backward from the passion narratives in search of lost truth. One scholar, for instance, envisions a political Jesus who, perhaps in league with Barabbas, launched a violent attack against the Temple. Reacting to this zealous action, the high priests, inclined toward the political status quo, handed Jesus over to Pilate, who in turn would not have hesitated to condemn the incendiary revolutionary. This interpretation construes Mark's narrative as a conscious depoliticization of Jesus' actions and intentions, in response to the Jewish War (66–70 CE) and attendant hostilities to Jewish messianism. In my opinion, Christian sources do not so widely misconstrue the historical situation as this reconstruction suggests. While some of his contemporaries certainly considered Jesus a zealot, nothing in his ministry warrants this view that he was a revolutionary who condoned the use of violence. The proposed historical reconstruction cannot support its own weight.

Noncanonical Narratives

In addition to the canonical Gospels, certain noncanonical Christian texts from the first two centuries prove important to this discussion. On the one hand, these sources confirm the apologetic and legendary tendencies uncovered in the Synoptic Gospels. On the other hand, these sources yield details—of potentially valid historicity—not imparted in the canonical Gospels. Of first importance among these texts is the *Gospel of Peter*. This fragmentary Gospel, known in a sixth-century CE manuscript copy, was discovered in a tomb at Akhmim in Upper Egypt at the end of the nineteenth century. It appears in a Greek codex that the deceased evidently valued, since he wished to take it with him into the tomb. The small volume also contains other writings; one of these, a long fragment of the *Apocalypse of Peter,* attributes itself to the apostle Peter. Though the title "Gospel of Peter" does not appear on the fragment that concerns us, the fragment likely belongs to this Gospel—of which the title, but no text, was previously known to scholars—since the fragment employs the first person, "I," in passages that manifestly refer to this disciple. For a long time, scholars believed this Gospel to consist uniquely of a passion narrative, since the acephalous text (excerpted without its beginning) opens on Jesus' appearance before Pilate. But since that time, various fragments of the Gospel have been found; one of these, the Papyrus 4009 from Oxyrhynchus, recounts a saying that also appears in the Synoptic Gospels as part of Jesus' missionary discourse (see Matt. 10:16). Since the canonical Gospels place this discourse in the Galilean ministry of Jesus, it is likely that it falls in a similar place in the *Gospel of Peter*. This coherence suggests that this Gospel did in fact cover Jesus' entire ministry, not solely his death.

The *Gospel of Peter* unfolds a passion narrative at all points similar to those in the Synoptic Gospels, with an equivalent nature and equal historical value to its New Testament parallels. The narrative unfolds thus: after the scene in which Pilate washes his hands, Joseph of Arimathea, having learned that the Lord (such is Jesus' title throughout the text) is going to be crucified, expresses his wish to take charge of the body and sends this request to Pilate. The governor, as in Luke, is in league with Herod and gives his assent. The author then details all the humiliations Jesus endured, among them the crown of thorns, before turning to the crucifixion. The sequence of events in the crucifixion resembles that found in the canonical Gospels: the casting of lots for Jesus' garments, the estimation of Jesus by one of the thieves, the refusal to break Jesus' legs, the honey and vinegar offered to assuage the victim's thirst. Only two details are particular to this noncanonical portrait. First, the text affirms that Jesus seemed not to suffer—an impassability due more to Jesus' heroism than to his divine nature. Second, the text records a final cry parallel to, but different from, "My God, my God, why have you forsaken me?" (Mark 15:34): "My power, O power, thou hast forsaken me" (*Gos. Pet.* 19).[7] Although the text speaks of Jesus' elevation at this moment, this does not necessarily imply that the text is docetic in nature.[8] After all, every Gospel expresses the atrocious reality of Jesus' death by euphemisms (just as we ourselves do, in saying that someone "passed away"). The narrative then continues on to the deposition from the cross, the burial by Joseph of Arimathea, and the reaction of the Jews. On this last subject, the noncanonical Gospel has more to say than the canonical Gospels. Here, the Jews are shown to realize the tragic repercussions of their act, attributing to it even the fall of Jerusalem. This part of the narrative closes on the words of the disciple who must be Peter himself: "But I mourned with my fellows, and being wounded in heart we hid ourselves, for we were sought after by them as evildoers and as persons who wanted to set fire to the Temple. Because of all these things we were fasting and sat mourning and weeping night and day until

7. All citations of the *Gospel of Peter* are taken from Christian Maurer's translation in *New Testament Apocrypha*, vol. 1, ed. Wilhelm Schneemelcher, rev. ed. (Louisville, KY: Westminster/John Knox Press, 1991).

8. "Docetism" was a Christian heresy that refused the true incarnation of the Son of God, understanding instead that the humanity of Jesus and his sufferings existed only in appearance (in Greek, the verb *dokeô* means to seem, to appear, to judge, to estimate).

the sabbath" (*Gos. Pet.* 26–27). While the pairing of Pilate and Herod links the *Gospel of Peter* to Luke (Luke 23:6–12), the presence of guards at the tomb links it to Matthew (Matt. 27:62–66).

Whatever parallels may be found to the passion narratives of the canonical Gospels, the resurrection narrative told in the *Gospel of Peter* is unique unto itself. It is the sole resurrection narrative that has come down to us with any pretense to objectivity. For the first time, the resurrection itself is recounted (the canonical Gospels only tell two results of the resurrection, in the empty tomb and the later appearances), and the witnesses to this resurrection are not Jesus' disciples, but the guards who stand watch about the tomb. What these sentries see does not lack for grandeur: they watch two beings, angels evidently, enter the tomb and then exit from it upholding a third person, the Lord, still weak with his passion, yet already exalted by his resurrection. Though he staggers, Jesus surpasses his angel-aides by a good head's height. In this tableau, the author evidently means to show—as does the author of the Epistle to the Hebrews, from the same period—how Jesus towers in importance over even the angelic hosts (see Heb. 1:4). While the terrified guards run to tell Pilate the news, the women approach the tomb, find it open and empty, and are told of the resurrection by a beautiful young man, also an angel (this version of the empty-tomb story closely resembles the Synoptic narratives). After this, the fragmentary *Gospel of Peter* ends as it begins, with a lacuna. The text breaks off at the beginning of a resurrection appearance, narrated in the text's final words, "But I, Simon Peter, and my brother Andrew took our nets and went to the sea. And there was with us Levi, the son of Alphaeus, whom the Lord . . ." (*Gos. Pet.* 60).

This long, fragmentary passion narrative is neither more miraculous nor more legendary than the canonical narratives. Rather, it shows, like the others, the cohabitation in such narratives of memory and interpretation. The interpretations stem, on the one hand, from an apologetic necessity, from the desire to recuperate the worth, honor, and importance in the eyes of God of the man who seemed a failure in the tide of history; to establish a causal connection between the death of Jesus and the fall of Jerusalem; and to absolve Pilate of guilt without at the same time making him a believer in the yet-unborn Christianity. On the other hand, these interpretations show the impact of Scripture on the narrative: if the crowd rushes forward to drag Jesus away (*Gos. Pet.* 6), it does so to fulfill a prophecy of Isaiah (Isa. 59:7); similarly, when the Lord's enemies wish to pierce him with a reed (*Gos. Pet.* 9), their wish corresponds to a phrase from the prophet Zechariah (Zech. 12:10).[9]

Among later Christian documents, the *Acts of Pilate* deserves mention. Even could it be believed that Pilate himself, in the days of Christian antiquity, wrote a report on the "Jesus incident" to enlighten his superior, the emperor, the *Acts of Pilate* that comes down to us today, in diverse forms and languages, would still seem rather to be a Christian compilation. It is altogether likely that this compilation sought to counteract the harmful effects of a false, pagan *Acts of Pilate*, now lost, but composed to disprove Christian claims during the persecution under Diocletian in the early fourth century. The Christian *Acts of Pilate* can be read today for information about the beliefs held at the time of its composition, but not for information about the events that unfolded in Jerusalem around the year 30 CE.[10]

Jewish Sources

As far as Jewish sources are concerned, the testimonies of Josephus and the Talmud warrant consideration. Leaving aside the Slavonic version of the Jewish historian Josephus, with its Christian interpolations, we do find an allusion to Jesus' passion in Josephus's writings (approximately 37–100/110 CE). In book 18 of the *Jewish Antiquities*, Josephus evokes several incidents that took

---

9. John Dominic Crossan believed he detected behind the *Gospel of Peter* an archaic narrative from which originated all the canonical and noncanonical passion narratives (*The Cross that Spoke: The Origins of the Passion Narrative* [San Francisco: Harper & Row, 1988]). Few critics, however, have upheld his hypothesis.

10. Of the studies relating to the *Acts of Pilate*, I recommend the recent work by Rémi Gounelle and Zbigniew Izydorczyk, *L'Évangile de Nicodème*, Apocryphes 9 (Turnhout: Brepols, 1997).

place in Palestine under the government of Pontius Pilate. He then presents the case of Jesus. What follows is the text referred to as the *Testimonium Flavianum*:

> About this time there lived Jesus, a wise man, if indeed one ought to call him a man. For he was one who wrought surprising feats and was a teacher of such people as accept the truth gladly. He won over many Jews and many of the Greeks. He was the Messiah. When Pilate, upon hearing him accused by men of the highest standing amongst us, had condemned him to be crucified, those who had in the first place come to love him did not give up their affection for him. On the third day he appeared to them restored to life, for the prophets of God had prophesied these and countless other marvelous things about him. And the tribe of the Christians, so called after him, has still to this day not disappeared.[11]

It is unlikely that a Jewish author wrote this text as it now stands (note, for instance, the reference to Christ's divinity, the admission of Jesus' messianic role, and the assertion of the resurrection). Though the entire passage could be a Christian interpolation, more probably it is in part authentic. Josephus could well have mentioned Jesus, the wise teacher, worker of miracles, and spiritual master. Likely, he would next have mentioned the crucifixion of the Nazarene, the result of Pilate's sentence, itself the result of the Jewish authorities' denunciation. Josephus's testimony probably would have finished with a mention of the Christian community that still remained active in his day. An authentic text along these lines evidently bore various alterations at the hand of later Christians, alterations easily attributable to this intervening hand.

An Israeli scholar, Shlomo Pines, has brought critical attention

---

11. Josephus, *Jewish Antiquities* 18.3 §63–64, trans. Louis H. Feldman (Cambridge, MA: Harvard University Press, 1965).

to an Arabic version of the *Testimonium Flavianum* preserved in the work of a tenth-century Christian historian, Agapius, whose universal history was widely known, edited, and even translated. The same account preserved in this work reappears almost identically in another universal history, by the Coptic Christian historian al-Makīn (thirteenth century). This admittedly late version is nevertheless of interest, for it appears less influenced by Christian doctrines than the earlier Greek text. In fact, it rather resembles the reconstruction of the original *Testimonium* offered above. This late Arabic text may preserve a fair measure of Josephus's original text. Although the chance of some Christian interpolation must be admitted even here, these interpolations are certainly fewer in number than in the Greek text. The account of Jesus' messianic nature in the Arabic text, for instance, seems to prove this point. In English translation, this *Testimonium* reads:

> At this time there was a wise man who was called Jesus. And his conduct was good, and [he] was known to be virtuous. And many people from among the Jews and the other nations became his disciples. Pilate condemned him to be crucified and to die. And those who had become his disciples did not abandon his doctrine [Pines prefers to retain here the variant found in al-Makīn, "his discipleship"]. They reported that he had appeared to them three days after his crucifixion and that he was alive; accordingly [al-Makīn reads "and perhaps this [man]"], he was perhaps the Messiah concerning whom the prophets have recounted wonders.[12]

In this version, the argument that Jesus was the Messiah seems to derive from either Josephus or the disciples. On the whole, Professor Pines's discovery confirms both the presence of alterations in the Greek text of the *Testimonium* and the authenticity of at least some part of the Greek text.[13]

12. Shlomo Pines, *An Arabic Version of the Testimonium Flavianum and Its Implications* (Jerusalem: Israeli Academy of Sciences and Humanities, 1971), 16.
13. Following Pines's discovery, many important studies have treated Josephus's

The historical interest of this account lies in the fact that it does not mention a trial of Jesus before the Sanhedrin, but only the condemnation by Pilate. Thus, while the Arabic version of the *Testimonium* does not mention the participation of the Jews in Jesus' trial, the Greek text, on the contrary, does refer to the denunciation of Jesus by Jewish authorities. The Greek text seems more faithful to the original on this point than the Arabic version. In each case, however, the death sentence comes from the Roman governor.[14]

Of rabbinical sources, only a single passage need be mentioned here. In the Babylonian Talmud, we read a *baraita* of the *Sanhedrin* tractate dating from the second century CE: "[I]t was taught: On the eve of the Passover, Yeshu [one manuscript adds "of Nazareth"] was hanged. For forty days before the execution took place, a herald went forth and cried, 'He is going forth to be stoned because he has practiced sorcery and enticed Israel to apostasy. Any one who can say anything in his favour, let him come forward and plead on his behalf.' But since nothing was brought forward in his favour he was hanged on the eve of the Passover!"[15]

Some have argued, by virtue of this passage's apologetic tone, that it lacks all historical validity. The reference to the herald does indeed emphasize Jesus' culpability and a respect for the legal process; as such, it might not be historically accurate. The hanging of a body after stoning also remains enigmatic. The mention

---

account; see in particular James Carleton Paget, "Some Observations on Josephus and Christianity," *JTS* 52 (2001): 539–624; Alice Whealey, *Josephus on Jesus: The Testimonium Flavianum Controversy from Late Antiquity to Modern Times*, Studies in Biblical Literature 36 (Bern: Peter Lang, 2003).

14. In another passage from the *Jewish Antiquities* (20.9.1 §200), Josephus recounts the execution of James by order of the high priest Annas. In order to specify to which James his account refers, Josephus adds "the brother of Jesus, called the Christ." The text, though considered authentic, does not add any new information about Jesus' death.

15. *Sanhedrin* 6.1 (or 43a by a different demarcation of the text); the edition cited here is the *Hebrew-English Edition of the Babylonian Talmud*, ed. I. Epstein, trans. Jacob Shachter and H. Freedman (London: Soncino Press, 1969).

of the Jewish punishment of stoning likely responds to the rabbis' difficulty in accepting that an uncircumcised man (Pilate) should have regulated, by crucifixion, a problem internal to Judaism. On the other hand, the date of the execution, which confirms the date in John's account, seems of solid historical value; so too do the grievances noted: sorcery (of which Jesus is often accused during the Galilean ministry in the Synoptic Gospels) and sedition (a grievance brought before Pilate by the Jews in Luke 23:2).[16]

Pagan Sources

Two quite valuable pagan texts allude to Jesus' passion. Tacitus, in his *Annals*, makes mention of the Roman fire and the persecution under Nero (15.44). He then explains the meaning of the word "Christian" as rooted in "Christus, the founder of the name," who "had undergone the death penalty in the reign of Tiberius, by sentence of the procurator, Pontius Pilatus."[17] Though it does not reveal anything new, this text seems not to rely on either Jewish or Christian sources and it thus confirms Jesus' existence and the reality of Pilate's sentence.

Finally, in a private Syriac letter, an otherwise unknown Syrian Stoic, Mara Bar Sarapion, writes to his son, a student at Edessa, enumerating the misfortunes that befall those who unjustly condemn virtuous men. After his exposition on the examples of Socrates and Pythagoras, he mentions the case of Jesus:

16. Another rabbinic text has often been cited: "Said R. Abbahu, 'If a man should tell you, "I am God," he is lying. If he says, "I am the son of man," in the end he will regret it. "For I shall go up to heaven"—Has he said, and will he not do it?' (Num 23:19)" (Jerusalem Talmud, *Taanit* 2:1, or by an alternate demarcation of the text 2.650.59; the edition cited here is *The Talmud of the Land of Israel*, vol. 18, trans. Jacob Neusner [Chicago: University of Chicago Press, 1982]). If this text references Jesus Christ, it needs to be understood in the context of the polemic between the synagogue and the church, rather than in the context of Jesus' life. It would seem then to reflect Jewish hostility to the christological claims of the church.

17. Tacitus, *Annals* 15.44, trans. John Jackson (Cambridge, MA: Harvard University Press, 1951).

For what advantage did the Athenians gain by the murder of Socrates, the recompense of which they received in famine and pestilence? Or the people of Samos by the burning of Pythagoras, because in one hour their country was entirely covered with sand? Or the Jews by the death of their wise king, because from that same time their kingdom was taken away? For with justice did God make recompense to the wisdom of these three: for the Athenians died of famine; and the Samians were overwhelmed by the sea without remedy; and the Jews, desolate and driven from their own kingdom, are scattered throughout every country. Socrates is not dead, because of Plato; neither Pythagoras, because of the statue of Juno; nor the Wise King, because of the laws which he promulgated.[18]

This author, writing at the end of the first century or the beginning of the second, knows of Jesus' death. He also knows that the title "king"—which plays a significant role in Mark 15 and John 18—was attributed to this Nazarene. He knows further that the impetus for Jesus' crucifixion lay with the Jews. It is possible, however, that Mara Bar Sarapion owes his information to a source sympathetic with growing Christianity. After all, does he not also link Jesus' fate to the fall of Jerusalem?

Conclusion

An analysis of the traditions contained in the New Testament uncovers a faith-confession centered on the cross and resurrection; it further reveals a kerygmatic message directed to the Jews, highlighting both Pilate's role in ordering Jesus' crucifixion (after the denunciation of the Jewish authorities) and the resurrection of Jesus enacted by God; and finally, it discloses a liturgical schema that narrates how Jesus, handed over to the Jewish and then pagan

---

18. Translation and commentary of Mara Bar Sarapion's letter in *Spicilegium Syriacum*, trans. William Cureton (London: Rivingtons, 1855), 73–74.

authorities, was crucified and raised from the dead. These three structural elements are not only traditional, but also ancient. It should not be assumed that the briefest of these—the confession of faith—is the origin of the others. For each schema responds to a different exigency, either to confess belief, to convince the circumcised, or to celebrate the faith. Jewish and pagan sources, evidently, do not share these same aims, but they do confirm certain points key to the narrative itself. First of all, Jesus existed; no one attempts to deny this. He was executed following a death sentence issued by Pilate (Josephus, Tacitus). The Jewish authorities were not unaware of this sentence (Greek text of Josephus, Mara Bar Sarapion, Babylonian Talmud). Beyond the statements and stories of the disciples, issued in faith, no non-Christian text affirms the resurrection of Jesus.

Chapter Two

Methodological Starting Point

J esus suffered a Roman, not a Jewish, punishment. The best sources prove unanimous on this point: whereas James, the brother of the Lord, was stoned by order of the Sanhedrin in 62, during the interregnum between the death of Festus and the coming of Albinus, Jesus was crucified by order of the Roman governor Pilate, who was present in Jerusalem to dispel any disturbances that might have arisen in connection with the Passover feast.[1] Jewish law contained no provision for crucifixion, itself a Roman penalty imported from the Orient.[2]

The condemnation of Jesus by Pilate, attested to by independent, ancient sources, is a historically established fact. In truth, it

---

1. An inscription, found in Caesarea in 1961, makes mention of Pilate, designating him by the title "prefect." This inscription seems to confirm the scholarly claim that the governor of a procuratorial province, often of the knightly order, would not have received the title "procurator" until the reign of Claude; see Jerry Vardaman, "A New Inscription Which Mentions Pilate as Prefect," *JBL* 81 (1962): 70–71; Adrian Nicholas Sherwin-White, *Roman Society and Roman Law in the New Testament* (Oxford: Clarendon, 1963), 6; Alvaro D'Ors, "Epigrafia juridica griega y romana (VIII)," *Studia et Documenta Historiae et Juris* 32 (1966): 472, and "Epigrafia juridica griega y romana (IX)," ibid., 35 (1969): 522 (bibliography); H. Volkmann, "Die Pilatus Inschrift von Caesarea Maritima," *Gymnasium* 75 (1968): 124–35.

2. The capital punishment of crucifixion has been examined in depth by Martin Hengel, *Crucifixion in the Ancient World and the Folly of the Message of the Cross*, trans. John Bowden (London: SCM Press, 1977).

25

is the best established fact of Jesus' life, one upheld by all contemporary scholars, both Jewish and Christian.[3] If the first Christians professed Jesus' crucifixion, it is because the event really took place. Practitioners of a new faith would never have invented such an end, one that shocked equally Jews and pagans. Nor did any Jewish expectation focus on the Messiah's redemptive death, much less a death on a cross. For, according to Jewish law, the one hung on a tree is cursed (Deut. 21:22–23; see Gal. 3:13). True, this curse originally referred to those condemned to death by Jewish tribunals, especially the victims of death by stoning, for their corpses were hung from a tree until nightfall. But later rabbinic thought linked the state of the crucified with that of the stoned. Crucifixion was equally troubling to Greek and Roman sensibilities. According to Cicero, who seems to voice the general opinion, "the very word 'cross' should be far removed not only from the person of a Roman citizen, but even from his thoughts, his eyes and his ears."[4]

Jesus' crucifixion, then, was accomplished by Pilate's command. But what charge did the Roman governor bring against him? An answer comes by way of the *titulus*, the inscription placed above the cross, which announced the grievance held against the condemned.[5] Indicating the *causa poenae*—the cause for punishment—on a panel either hung about the neck of the condemned or carried before the condemned on the way to execution is a custom well attested to in Latin authors (see Suetonius, *Caligula*, 32, and *Domitian*, 10). The four Gospels all agree that, according to

---

3. Ernst Bammel, the editor of *The Trial of Jesus: Cambridge Studies in Honour of C. F. D. Moule* (London: SCM Press, 1970), contends that the choice of crucifixion as penalty might be better explained with reference to the grievance held against Jesus (political in nature) than with reference to the nationality of those who judged and condemned Jesus (a Roman tribunal).

4. *In Defense of Rabirius* 5.16, in *The Speeches*, trans. H. Grose Hodge (New York: G. P. Putnam's Sons, 1927).

5. See Peter Egger, *"Crucifixus sub Pontio Pilato". Das "crimen" Jesu von Nazareth im Spannungsfeld römischer und jüdischer Verwaltungs- und Rechtsstrukturen*, NTAbh,, NS 32 (Münster: Aschendorff, 1997); Ellis Rivkin, *What Crucified Jesus? Messianism, Pharisaism, and the Development of Christianity* (New York: UAHC Press, 1997).

the *titulus*, Pilate condemned Jesus as a messianic pretender: in each of the four Gospels, the phrase "King of the Jews" appears on the *titulus* at the top of the cross.[6]

Several indications confirm the likelihood of this record's historical validity. That sacred authors did not invent this grievance may be argued from the fact that the title "King of the Jews" never became a christological title of the ancient church. If, instead of this phrase, the evangelists reported "Savior of mankind" or "Lord of the Universe" as the inscription on the *titulus*, there would be good reason to distrust their testimony. But this is not the case. Moreover, Mara Bar Sarapion's testimony confirms that the "royalty" of Jesus played a role in his trial.[7] The theme of Jesus' royalty also figures centrally in both Mark 15 and John 18, from the moment that Pilate enters the scene.

A Roman tribunal thus condemned Jesus for messianic pretensions and, no doubt, for having provoked, through these pretensions, agitation in the crowd. Luke adds the corollary grievance of sedition: "They began to accuse him, saying, 'We found this man perverting our nation, forbidding us to pay taxes to the emperor, and saying that he himself is the Messiah, a king'" (Luke 23:2). These grievances, which led to Jesus' crucifixion, form the starting point from which our understanding of the events of the passion narrative will unfold.

6. Mark 15:26, "The King of the Jews"; Matt. 27:37, "This is Jesus, the King of the Jews"; Luke 23:38, "This is the King of the Jews"; John 19:19, "Jesus the Nazorean, the King of the Jews."

7. The Greek text of Josephus's account similarly affirms this importance, asserting Jesus' messianic nature. While this text was certainly edited by Christian copyists, the Arabic version, as we saw earlier, may also suggest that Jesus' disciples believed him to be the Messiah (see above, pp. 19–21).

Chapter Three

The Unfolding of Events

If Jesus was condemned for messianic pretensions and sedition, two further questions arise: How did Pilate come to hold these grievances? And were these grievances justified? To answer these questions, we first must briefly trace Jesus' own intentions, in order to reconstruct how events unfolded during Holy Week.

The heart of Jesus' message, and thus the key to uncovering his intentions, emerges in his teachings on the imminent coming of the kingdom of God. Jesus announced the establishment of God's kingdom on earth and, in so doing, he spread not only a religious message of great scope, but also a political one. His interest in God's kingdom distinguishes Jesus from groups like the Essenes, who withdrew from the world to order their community life under the watchful eye of God in the desert. Jesus, by contrast, wandered the pathways of Galilee, then the streets of Jerusalem. In these wanderings, Jesus evoked the love of the God who will establish his reign on earth and Jesus recalled, through his teachings, the commands of the Lord who stretched out his arm to save. This message—and the signs that accompanied it—astonished crowds, troubled the Pharisees, and shocked the Sadducees. Like any prophetic and apocalyptic message, Jesus' preaching also contained an ethical component. As a teacher, Jesus advanced an ethic of freedom, responsibility, and, above all, love for one's neighbor. This message of personal involvement shook social convention, creating a system that engages entirely the individual will: the coming kingdom, Jesus proclaimed, demands a willingness to serve that will not balk before suffering.[1]

This particular message became the basis from which Jesus interpreted the Law, critiqued the oral tradition held dear by the scribes, and crafted a new hierarchy of values that disrupted the comfortable situation of the high clerical orders. He crossed taboos, ate with sinners, kept company with women, and debated with the uncircumcised. He possessed the allure of an incendiary prophet, a preacher of repentance, and a gentle companion who never ceased giving thanks to God for the beauty of creation. In all these things, Jesus proves himself a man beyond characterization, neither a true rabbi, nor a true prophet, nor a true teacher. Provoking admiration, he intrigued many and, intriguing many, he also provoked in some great anxiety.

It often falls to those who, like Jesus, do not fit into the established framework to be misunderstood. Zealous intentions, for instance, can easily be read into certain ambiguous actions Jesus performed, such as his entry into Jerusalem (Mark 11:1–11) and the purification of the Temple (Mark 11:15–17). Some of his enigmatic sayings, like "I came to bring fire to the earth" (Luke 12:49) and "I have not come to bring peace, but a sword" (Matt. 10:34), can fall subject to similar misconstructions. These interpretations of zealotry do have a perceptible origin. After all, one of the Twelve was originally a zealot (Luke 6:15), and some of the disciples (including Judas?) hoped that Jesus would reestablish Israel (Luke 24:21; Acts 1:6). But Jesus himself advocated a different way: he demanded of men and women weakness and poverty, as well as responsibility and obedience to God. He

---

1. Some recent studies of the historical Jesus—those designated, for ease, under the rubric of the "third quest for the historical Jesus"—deny the apocalyptic dimension of Jesus' message, perceiving a rather extreme opposition between the apocalyptic and the ethical orientation. These studies argue that Jesus' identity corresponds more to a wisdom teacher than to a prophet of the last days; see, for example, John Dominic Crossan, *The Historical Jesus: The Life of a Mediterranean Jewish Peasant* (San Francisco: Harper Collins, 1991).

united himself to the disempowered, lifted up the lowly, and called his disciples to follow the way of suffering and renunciation. Though he announced the coming of a powerful kingdom and the reconstitution of the person in this life (not merely the salvation of the soul in the beyond), he never undertook to establish this kingdom or this salvation by human force. That fulfillment, according to his teaching, could be accomplished only by the beneficent God. He called on humans to put their trust in God by a movement at once passive and active: they must leave God alone to act, yet they alone can hand their lives over to God's accomplishing power.

Despite potential misconstructions, then, Jesus was no zealot. He never sought to seize the sword or overthrow the Romans or destroy the Temple or become here below the King of the Jews. John the Baptist bore only religious intentions, yet he died a martyr at Herod's hand, for Herod feared his prophetic message might have political repercussions (see Josephus, *Jewish Antiquities* 18.5.2 §116–19). So too things went with Jesus. The man was misunderstood, and the message—for all its popular success—was misinterpreted.

Given this tendency toward misunderstanding, is it nevertheless possible to retrace what happened in Jerusalem, to know how things went awry? It is possible, to a degree. A critical study of the four Gospel narratives enables a hypothetical reconstruction of the historical events leading to Jesus' death. Such a reconstruction occupies the remainder of this chapter.

This reconstruction begins when Jesus enters Jerusalem. The chronology given in Mark, which places this entry one week before Passover, is certainly redacted. Historically, the event could have occurred earlier. Jesus' moment of entry into the city, unlike the triumphal scene painted by the Gospel narratives, was surely a modest one, celebrated only by his followers. The early church transformed the simple event into one worthy of the Messiah's glorious entry into his holy, and wholly enthusiastic, city (see Mark 11:1–11 and parallels).

The purification of the Temple, despite its placement in John's Gospel (John 2:13–22), must have taken place during this final period of Jesus' life. It should be seen in terms of a symbolic act, like those occasionally performed by the prophets of old. In this case, the prehistory of the Gospel texts (see especially Mark 11:16) suggests that Jesus' violent action called symbolically for a radical reform of the Temple. However wide-reaching the symbolism, the action itself must have retained a limited scope. Otherwise, the sanctuary guards and Roman troops (stationed at the Antonia fortress just steps away) surely would have intervened to reestablish order. Yet Jesus' disruptive action would still have proven vastly irritating to those high priests who constituted the Temple administration—a priestly aristocracy with Sadducean leanings—and to whom fell all its rich profits.

Jesus awoke also the animosity of the scribes through his teachings and the resultant quarrels incited with this group while he was in Jerusalem. In fact, the scribes, Pharisees for the most part, probably had a fair awareness of Jesus and his message prior to his arrival in Jerusalem, since several of them had already crossed swords with him in Galilee (see Mark 3:22–27).

As the time for the Passover celebration approached, the atmosphere in Jerusalem would have grown tense. Zealous groups moved restlessly throughout the region. These groups play a large, if hidden, role in the Gospel narratives: in qualifying Barabbas as a "rebel," the Synoptic evangelists surely follow the same impulse as Josephus, denoting Barabbas, through this appellation, as a zealot, a partisan of violence. Though the text in Mark is not altogether clear on this point (see Mark 15:7), Barabbas was likely arrested in company with other subversive elements over the course of a riot. The "thieves" of the cross, perhaps also zealots, were probably arrested during the same uprising. In the midst of this turmoil, Jesus appeared, and the Jewish authorities, for fear of Roman retaliation, sought to reinstate order and calm. The Gospel of John, often faithful to historical detail, accurately depicts the sort of logic the Jewish authorities must have followed in pursuing Jesus: "If we let him go on like this, everyone will believe in him, and the Romans will come and destroy both our holy place and our nation" (John 11:48). The Jewish authorities had good reason for wishing to retain order. In seeking to avoid further disturbance, they believed they were accomplishing their duty.

The means they used to attain this legitimate end proved less honorable. The Jewish leaders plotted how best to arrest Jesus surreptitiously; hence the night, hence the traitor. Why did they employ these precautions? They probably seemed necessary on account of the crowd, which was widely in sympathy with the Galilean. Scholars have too long neglected, in discussions of Jesus' trial, to attribute due significance to the part played by the Jerusalem crowd.

From the crowd, the action moves to a few followers gathered around a table. A solid tradition, attested to by independent texts, places that meal we now call the Last Supper on the night when Jesus was handed over (Mark 14:22–25 and parallels, as well as 1 Cor. 11:23–27). External details, such as the date, the type of meal, and so on, vary from source to source and cannot be determined with any precision. Some details of the tradition, on the other hand, can be claimed with relative certainty: besides the linking of the Last Supper and the arrest to the same night, the presence of the elements (bread and wine) and the utterance of some explicative words concerning them are well established. The paschal tone that reigned around the table must have contributed further to the sense of imminent drama.[2] This drama unfolds next in the garden: the Epistle to the Hebrews (Heb. 5:7) and the Gospel of John (John 12:27–28) both add weight to the tradition set forth by the Synoptics concerning Gethsemane. Although, in their present forms, the Gospel narratives display signs of reworking by the

---

2. The traditional date of the Last Supper, fixed at Thursday evening, has been contested by Annie Jaubert (*Date of the Last Supper* [Staten Island, NY: Alba House, 1965]). Using the solar calendar of the Qumran community and the fixed feast days it implies, the French exegete has argued that Jesus' Last Supper must be dated to the Tuesday evening of Holy Week, which was the date of the Essene paschal meal. This transposition manages to reconcile the divergent chronologies of the Synoptic Gospels and the Gospel of John. Though this exciting hypothesis garnered much attention, it has not gathered the support of many exegetes. While the existence of two conflicting calendars in first-century CE Palestine is certain, it is less certain that Jesus would have adhered to the Essene model.

early church—with an eye to the Hebrew Bible, under a parenetic impulse—these narratives do contain an ancient tradition that describes Jesus' prayer in his moment of trial.

The arrest itself was the work of the Jews. The sources suggest no conspiring between Pilate and the high priest about the arrest, for, had they so conspired, each party would have sent its own escort. Only the Johannine narrative mentions both a detachment of soldiers and a band of Jewish police, and it manifestly reports a legendary detail and not a historical one (John 18:3, 12). This particular detail aims to show how much human force was required to arrest the Son of God. Thus John shows Jesus assenting to his own arrest in the face of the soldiers' amazement: when Jesus merely identifies himself, the whole armed troop falls back, faces to the ground (John 18:6). Such details are legendary, not historical.

What happened next? Did the Sanhedrin really meet? Were there two sessions of interrogation, at midnight and at dawn? What grievances were launched against Jesus? Threats against the Temple? Messianic pretensions? Did the Sanhedrin condemn Jesus to death? Did it have the jurisdiction for such a sentence? The Synoptics do not agree on the answers to these questions. Beyond even the problem of such inconsistencies, however, further difficulties arise of both a historical and juridical nature.[3] Let us pause, therefore, over these questions and their difficult answers.

The majority of our knowledge about the Sanhedrin comes from a tractate of the Mishnah. This particular tractate, titled *Sanhedrin*, was written from a Pharisaic perspective, during the period following the fall of Jerusalem. We thus know little of the Sanhedrin prior to 70, little from that period of concern for these questions, when the Sadducees held all between their hands.

---

3. See Weddig Fricke, *Standrechtlich gekreuzigt. Person und Prozess des Jesus aus Galiläa* (Frankfurt: Mai Verlag, 1986); Dale M. Foreman, *Crucify Him: A Lawyer Looks at the Trial of Jesus* (Grand Rapids: Zondervan, 1990), 107–44.

A new hypothesis has been advanced that the Sanhedrin, such as it can be reconstructed from the later testimony of the Mishnah, did not yet exist during the period that concerns us here.[4] Instead, the argument runs, there was, on the one hand, a council of elders (similar to the *boulê* or *gerousia* of the Greeks) and, on the other, a pair of assemblies—one consultative, one arbitrative—that met as circumstance or necessity dictated. The composition or convocation of these two assemblies depended uniquely on the power and decision of a single leader. This hypothesis asserts that the Gospels and Josephus alike confer the name "Sanhedrin" on these two assemblies, perhaps conflating them under the influence of the later institution called by that name. I would argue, however, that when the first Christian authors and the Jewish historian speak of the Sanhedrin, they witness to an institutional reality already in place by the first century of the Common Era. I contend that the Sanhedrin already existed and exercised extensive power, especially in judiciary matters. For certain customs detailed in the Mishnah bear the mark of having been in practice for some time, as, for instance, that no judgment can be made after a single day of deliberations or that no trials can be held on the Sabbath, feast days, days of preparation, and so on.

If Jesus was tried before the Sanhedrin, then right penal procedure must have been disregarded (both the prohibitions mentioned above would seem to have been ignored in his case). But was there really a trial before this Jewish assembly? And, to add a subsidiary question of some significance, did the Sanhedrin possess, in the first century CE, the right to condemn a criminal to death?

Some scholars contend that the Sanhedrin did possess, during this period, the authority to pronounce capital sentences and to see them through to execution. Given this view, these scholars conclude that Jesus could not have appeared before the Jewish tribunal since, historically, Jesus was executed under a Roman punishment, one ordered by Pilate. In support of this argument, these scholars further allude to the respect the Roman establishment

---

4. See James S. McLaren, *Power and Politics in Palestine: The Jews and the Governing of Their Land 100 BC–AD 70*, JSNTSup 63 (Sheffield: JSOT Press, 1991).

maintained toward the autonomy of local groups,[5] citing a significant number of executions ordered by the Sanhedrin in the first century CE. But the cases they cite do not prove conclusive. Such cases more likely reflect abuses committed by the Sanhedrin in its desire to recuperate the lost right of capital sentencing. The opportunity for such recuperation would have been particularly ripe when the procurator was absent. As for the autonomy of the Sanhedrin, it must be remembered that Herod the Great severely limited the reach of its power. Furthermore, in a province as agitated as Judea at this time, the Roman governor would certainly not have conferred upon the Sanhedrin a right he withheld even from his immediate inferiors. In support of this counterargument stand both Josephus's testimony, which asserts that the Roman governor arrived in the province armed by right of the sword,[6] and the testimony of the Fourth Gospel, which places in the mouth of the Jewish authorities the phrase "We are not permitted to put anyone to death" (John 18:31).

Nor does the continuance of the prohibition on uncircumcised men entering into the sanctuary of the Jerusalem Temple beyond the court of the Gentiles detract from the argument just made.[7] The Romans granted the Jews an exceptional privilege in allowing them to apply this prohibition. Moreover, the specific application of the prohibition remains unclear: would a Roman or a Greek, guilty of a crime, still have had to appear in front of a tri-

---

5. The First Cyrene Edict signals that the criminal jury made up of Roman citizens was reformed under Augustus to be half constituted by Greeks. This instance does not breach the exclusive power the Roman authority held in capital cases, however, for the governor was to decide if he wished to hear a given affair personally or to hand it over to the jury. In any case, Judea, unlike Cyrenaica, was not composed of free cities. Its status more closely resembled that of Sicily, where the cities were subject to Rome, and where capital trials fell exclusively to the Roman governor; see Fernand de Visscher, *Les édits d'Auguste découverts à Cyrène* (Louvain: Bureau du Recueil, Bibliothèque de l'Université, 1940; repr., Osnabrück: O. Zeller, 1965).

6. Josephus, *The Jewish War* 2.8.1 §117.

7. Engraved panels located at the edge of forbidden areas warned passersby of this prohibition. The text of these prohibitions comes down through Philo and Josephus. Excavations have also uncovered two examples of the panels themselves, revealing them to be stone blocks covered in a highly readable inscription.

bunal before being executed? If so, would this appearance have been before the Sanhedrin, or before the Roman governor? Finally, who then performed the execution, the Temple police or Roman troops?

Other historians consider that the Sanhedrin retained during this period its right to pronounce capital sentences, but that it had lost the right to execute them. Others still, bearing in mind the *ordo iudiciorum publicorum* procedure, deem that the Sanhedrin, acting as jury, reached a judgment of Jesus' guilt, while Pilate, as magistrate, pronounced the punishment on the basis of its verdict. According to both of these theories, Jesus would have been tried before the Sanhedrin. Pilate, having in the first instance the power to execute the death sentence or, in the second, both to pronounce and execute the sentence, would also have had the right to reopen Jesus' case to further examination—a right the governor evidently retained. Whichever view of the Sanhedrin's power is correct, both hypotheses account for the two successive trials reported in the sources, one before the Sanhedrin, one before Pilate.

Critical exegesis of the Gospel sources brings some light to bear on these two variant hypotheses of the Sanhedrin's role in Jesus' trial. Of the four Gospels, neither Luke nor John makes any mention of a death sentence pronounced by the Sanhedrin (see Luke 22:71–23:1 and John 18:24, 28). Matthew and Mark, however, do mention such a death sentence. Yet in Matthew the verb "to condemn" does not figure in the scene in which Jesus appears before the Sanhedrin, it appears only in a later passage (Matt. 27:3). While Mark uses the expression "condemn to death" in one of the passion predictions (Mark 10:33), as well as in the scene of Jesus' appearance before the Sanhedrin, the phrase proves ambiguous in this last formulation.[8] Since the Gospels display the tendency to augment the responsibility of the Jews, it seems reasonable to

8. In his article "Utilitas Crucis. Observations sur les récits du procès de Jésus dans les évangiles canoniques," Elias Bickermann translates Mark 14:64 as "Tous se prononcèrent contre lui comme ayant mérité la mort" ("They all pronounced against him as having merited death"), suggesting that Mark does not intend by this phrase to evoke the solemn pronouncement of the death sentence (*RHR* 112 [1935]: 182–83).

argue, in this instance, that Luke and John approach historical truth more closely than Mark and Matthew. Had the Sanhedrin condemned Jesus to death, the Gospel sources would have recorded, probably even augmented, the role their judgment played. In the absence of such a testimony, a different conclusion must be reached.

The Sanhedrin, in my estimation, only investigated Jesus' case. From this investigation, the Sanhedrin deemed Jesus deserving of the most extreme punishment. And since it did not then possess the right to pronounce or execute a capital sentence, it sent a delegation to denounce Jesus to the Roman governor, who did.

Before taking up the trial before Pilate, let us attempt to determine how exactly this first phase of Jesus' trial played out. Despite some discrepancies, the Gospels have in common that they all indicate a double appearance of Jesus before the Jewish authorities (the fragment from the *Gospel of Peter* begins later, with the appearance before Pilate). Matthew and Mark signal a long meeting of the Sanhedrin during the night, followed by a short session in the morning. In Luke, Jesus is taken to the house of the high priest in the evening and appears before the Sanhedrin the next morning. And John recounts Jesus' interrogation first by Annas, then by Caiaphas. Given these concurring accounts, some sort of double appearance or two-part interrogation seems historically probable. The functioning high priest, Caiaphas, or the former high priest, Annas, father-in-law to Caiaphas and a powerful figure in the Sanhedrin, likely questioned Jesus shortly after his arrest and shortly before the meeting of the Sanhedrin.

The surprising mention of the fire and the crowd of servants around it in the scene of Peter's denial probably indicates that, for this interrogation, the high priest was surrounded by a few influential members of the Sanhedrin, who came accompanied by servants. Peter's denial itself seems historically authentic. It is hard to imagine the church, built in part on the pillar of this apostle, inventing this humiliating episode. The denial surely occurred at the moment of this first interrogation, as Mark and John recount, not during the meeting of the Sanhedrin.

What questions were put to Jesus at this time? It is impossible to know. The one potentially revelatory phrase from the Fourth Gospel, "then the high priest questioned Jesus about his disciples and about his teaching" (John 18:19), reflects John's theology more than any historical actuality.

As for the five episodes of abuse detailed in the Gospels, they surely derive from two actual instances, one at Jesus' exit from the interrogation by the high priest or his appearance before the Sanhedrin and the other at the close of the trial before Pilate. On the first occasion, Jesus is mocked as a prophet; on the second, he is ridiculed as a king.

The entire Sanhedrin probably met during the day, following Jesus' evening arrest and interrogation. Early in the morning, the assembly had Jesus brought forward. With what did it charge him? Since the Gospel of John says nothing in this respect, any information must come from the Synoptic Gospels. Before turning to those accounts, however, an important question arises: how exactly did early Christians learn the matter of this investigation? Conservative exegetes make reference to Joseph of Arimathea and Nicodemus, who would have been present, arguing further that assemblies of this sort never succeed in keeping their affairs secret. Critical exegetes, among which include this author, deem rather that, here as elsewhere, the Gospel narratives reflect the desire of the Christian community more than the historical reality.

The morning session seems to have unfolded in two periods. In the first period, the Sanhedrin needed to make a unanimous decision regarding Jesus' guilt. If unanimity could not be reached, a minority could challenge the high priest. Such was the situation when the high priest Ananus condemned James, brother of Jesus, without the complete approval of the Sanhedrin. One faction of the Sanhedrin brought a complaint before King Agrippa II, an opposing faction before the new procurator, Albinus, and Ananus lost his position for the trouble (see Josephus, *Jewish Antiquities* 20.9.1 §197–203). Caiaphas, the high priest during Jesus' case, maneuvered more successfully and avoided such an error, managing to remain in place for nineteen years (18–37 CE) by virtue of his diplomatic skill.

In order to establish the guilt of the accused, Caiaphas needed witnesses. To this end, he evidently brought forward those who could report on one of Jesus' sayings. The Gospels record a bit of this testimony: "This fellow said, 'I am able to destroy the temple of God and to build it in three days'" (Matt. 26:61). In fact, this one saying on the Temple reappears all over the New Testament, recurring in slightly divergent forms at the opening of John's Gospel (John 2:19) as well as in the Acts of the Apostles, in reference to Stephen: "We have heard him say that this Jesus the Nazorean will destroy this place and will change the customs that Moses handed on to us" (Acts 6:14). The saying was not, therefore, associated solely with Jesus' appearance before the Sanhedrin. For this reason, some scholars exclude it from discussions of the trial. Yet this exclusion is unnecessary; the saying's occurrence elsewhere need not negate the role it may have played in this investigation. It would be useful to know, however, why Mark characterizes this statement as part of the contradictory, false testimonies brought against Jesus. Perhaps he characterizes it thus under influence from the psalm, "For false witnesses have risen against me, and they are breathing out violence" (Ps. 27:12). Or perhaps it is because Jesus himself never claimed that he would destroy the Temple; he may simply have critiqued the Temple, announcing its eschatological destruction.

Either way, Jesus' attitude toward the Temple must have played a significant role in the interrogation. Four indications for this focus come to light: first, the incident of Jesus purifying the Temple, which must have been interpreted badly; second, Jesus' saying about the Temple, though the tenor of this remark is hard to reconstruct; third, Hebrew Bible precedents, in which prophets who critiqued the priestly order or foretold misfortune to the Temple suffered persecution and death (see Jer. 26:8–9, 20–23); and finally, parallels in Acts, in which the Jews reproach Stephen and Paul, Christ's disciples, for a similar attitude toward the Temple (Acts 6:14 and 21:28). Though the subject of the Temple was surely brought forward at this time, it is unlikely that the saying so precisely recorded in Matthew and Mark was actually pronounced. The Sanhedrin's unanimous judgment against

Jesus was likely determined by his entire prophetic message, understood by every faction of the Sanhedrin as an attack against what seemed the very heart of Judaism, namely, the Temple.

Yet Jesus' attitude toward the Temple, according to Matthew and Mark, was not sufficient to condemn him. The three Synoptics show that the Sanhedrin's condemnation is provoked immediately by Jesus' response to the high priest's question, "Are you the Messiah, the Son of the Blessed One?" (Mark 14:61 and parallels). This question opens the second phase of the interrogation, which centered on Jesus' own royal and messianic nature. For this interrogation, witnesses were no longer needed. Jesus would testify for himself.

In response to the high priest's question, "Are you the Messiah, the Son of the Blessed One?" (Mark 14:61 and parallels), only the Markan Jesus directly answers. There, he intones, "I am" (Mark 14:62). This answer surely presents a redactional interpretation, corresponding to the christology of Mark, in which Jesus reveals himself to be the Christ as he approaches the cross. Matthew and Luke report a more ambiguous answer: in Matthew, *su eipas*, "You have said so," or "It's you who says so" (Matt. 26:64); in Luke, "If I tell you, you will not believe" (Luke 22:67). From this discrepancy, the Synoptics fall into agreement on Jesus' next utterance. All three show Jesus to then pronounce his famous saying on the Son of Man: "You will see the Son of Man seated at the right hand of the Power, and coming with the clouds of heaven" (Mark 14:62 and parallels).[9] This response, the Synoptic Gospels concur, provoked the Sanhedrin's decision. On hearing these words, the Sanhedrin cried blasphemy and declared Jesus deserving of death.

Several puzzling points arise from this second phase of the interrogation. First, many false messiahs came forward in the first two centuries of the Common Era. Yet none of these other pretenders were charged with blasphemy. Second, it is difficult to

---

9. There may linger a remembrance of Jesus' appearance before the Sanhedrin in the rabbinic sentence quoted earlier (n. 16, page 22): "If he says, 'I am the son of man,' in the end he will regret it."

believe that Jesus, as Mark asserts, would have accepted the title "Messiah." He seems rather to have refused this title throughout his earthly ministry. Third, at the moment when the evangelists wrote, the debate about Jesus' messianic nature was beginning to divide Jews and Christians.[10] It seems likely, therefore, that the evangelists projected back into Jesus' life this stumbling block for the Judaism of their time. Fourth and last, the influence of the Hebrew Bible can be felt throughout this interrogation: Ps. 27:12 (false witnesses); Isa. 53:7 (the victim's silence); Ps. 110:1 (one seated at God's right hand); Dan. 7:13 (Son of Man). This strong scriptural presence hardly inspires confidence in the Gospel texts' historical authenticity here.

Given these complications, we would do well to question what exactly happened during this second phase of interrogation. Let it be clear, from the outset, that things must have followed a very different course than that related in the Synoptics. Having unanimously determined from a Jewish perspective Jesus' guilt as a false prophet (see Deut. 18:20), the Sanhedrin sought a grievance that would warrant the death sentence from a Roman perspective.[11] The Sanhedrin found this grievance in the political sphere. Political concerns still shine through the high priest's question, "Are you the Messiah, the Son of the Blessed One?" The high priest must have questioned Jesus' messianic pretensions and, in so doing, he also examined his political aims. The Synoptic Gospels, which must be correct on this point, report that Jesus did

---

10. Of course, at this time, the distinction remains internal to Judaism; Christians formed one sect—in the sociological sense of the term—among others, within the Jewish religion. The growing presence of pagans in Christian communities sped the division into two religions, Judaism and Christianity. Daniel Boyarin, in his recent work, correctly asserts that this distinction must not be imposed anachronistically. He has not, however, convinced this reader that the date of separation should be fixed ultimately in the fourth century; see Boyarin, *Dying for God: Martyrdom and the Making of Christianity and Judaism* (Stanford, CA: Stanford University Press, 1999); see also the work he recently completed, *Border Lines: The Partition of Judaeo-Christianity* (Philadelphia: University of Pennsylvania Press, 2004).

11. Or, if one contends that the Sanhedrin retained the right to pronounce capital sentences at this time, the Sanhedrin may simply have sought a ratification of its judgment by Pilate.

respond to this question. What was his response? It must have touched on the transcendent power of the Son of Man, a figure with whom Jesus probably did not identify himself. In giving this response, Jesus essentially refused to enter into the political schema that opposed Jews and Romans. "My kingdom is not from this world" (John 18:36) seems a Christian commentary, faithful in spirit, on Jesus' response to the Sanhedrin. Without identifying himself as the Son of Man, Jesus nevertheless linked his own ministry to the kingdom of God. This response sufficed for the Sanhedrin to condemn him: "Why do we still need witnesses?" (Mark 14:63 and parallels).

Mark and Matthew present the high priest as exclaiming at this moment, "You have heard his blasphemy!" (Mark 14:64; see Matt. 26:65). Great misunderstanding has grown around this single word, "blasphemy." While it is true that, in rabbinic law, the one who blasphemes is punishable by death, the word "blasphemy" specifically refers to the act of pronouncing God's name. Strictly speaking, then, Jesus has not blasphemed. In fact, his response to the high priest's question distinctly avoids speaking God's name by invoking instead the "Power." This circumlocution avails little, however, for in the first century the restrictive sense of "blasphemy" had not yet been imposed. "Blasphemy," at the time of Jesus' trial, could mean any serious attack on the Jewish religion. Thus the scribes could cry blasphemy as early as Mark 2:7, when Jesus dares to forgive the paralytic man. In this larger sense of the term, members of the Sanhedrin may well have cried blasphemy at Jesus' response to the high priest's question.[12]

The interrogations complete, the Sanhedrin unanimously agreed on Jesus' guilt. Since the time had passed when the Sanhedrin had the right to pronounce capital sentences, it sent a delegation to Pilate, to ensure that he would pronounce such a sentence.[13] With the Passover feast fast approaching, it was

12. Moreover, the Greek work *blasphêmia*, used here by Mark and Matthew, can refer to diverse offenses to men as well as to gods.

13. Or, the Sanhedrin sought to obtain Pilate's ratification and execution of the capital sentence it had already pronounced.

essential to act quickly. If the Jewish authorities wished to have the whole affair judged and completed that same day, they must have presented themselves to Pilate in the morning, during the hours when Roman magistrates worked.

One last remark is due before passing on to the trial before Pilate: it would be wrong to vilify the Sanhedrin, as has all too often been done. A traditional view holds that the Sanhedrin condemned Jesus for blasphemy, yet being unable to offer this grievance to Pilate, it dishonestly construed another, political grievance that would unleash Roman retribution. But the two grievances, in fact, were indissoluble in Jewish thought (see the parallel case of Paul in the Acts of the Apostles). In the eyes of the Sanhedrin, an attack within the religious sphere would lead inevitably to social and political disorder and would thus naturally disquiet the Romans.

To understand Pilate's intervention in Jesus' case requires visiting briefly certain aspects of Roman criminal law.[14] Even in Rome, at the outset of the Principate, the *quaestiones perpetuae* — juries composed of citizens, begun in the time of the Republic— continued to exist. Each of these juries judged a specific crime (extortion, sacrilege, murder, etc.) according to a precise law. While this "ordinary" justice (*ordo iudiciorum publicorum*) was still in practice, however, there began to develop—and not all at once, as was previously believed, but progressively—an administrative type of justice, called the *cognitio extra ordinem*. This justice was performed directly by the emperor, the Senate, or imperial functionaries (like provincial governors), who thereby acquired the functions of magistrate and judge. At first begun by necessity, for those cases not covered by the provisions of the *ordo*, this new type of justice and the new procedures that accompanied it slowly came to extend across all legal domains.[15]

---

14. See Peter Egger, "*Crucifixus sub Pontio Pilato*". *Das "crimen" Jesu von Nazareth im Spannungsfeld römischer und jüdischer Verwaltungs- und Rechtstrukturen*, NTAbh, NS 32 (Münster: Aschendorff, 1997); Francesco Amarelli and Francesco Lucrezi, *Il processo contro Gesù*, Quaestiones 2 (Naples: Jovene, 1999).

15. See Jean Gaudemet, *Institutions de l'Antiquité* (Paris: Sirey, 1967), 778ff.

The way these penal procedures played out in the Roman provinces proves quite pertinent to this study.[16] The procedure of the *ordo* was respected for some time in the senatorial provinces and probably also in the imperial provinces. There, the local juries generally were maintained. In the procuratorial provinces like Judea, by contrast, the *cognitio extra ordinem* of the governor—who in such instances represented the emperor—was the sole procedure used in cases of criminal law.

Yet capital trials were unique across the empire, in that capital sentencing was beyond the purview of the local powers in all provinces, including senatorial provinces. Capital cases always fell first to the governor. He then could decide to pursue the case himself, according to his proper *cognitio*, or to hand it over to a jury, if one existed.[17] In a province with free cities, like Cyrenaica, juries were normally established in the court, and the governor most likely would hand the case over to one of them. But in a subjugated province, like Judea, the governor seems always to have guarded sole rights over capital sentencing. Moreover, the governor would have been hard pressed, in Judea, to find enough Roman citizens to form a tribunal or enough with sufficient income to apply to become judge. Finally, it is notable that capital trials of aliens (namely, those subjects who were not Roman citizens—like Jesus, but unlike Paul) ordinarily were handled by the governor, according to the *cognitio extra ordinem*, not by jury, according to the *ordo*.

All the above is offered with a double warning, the first relating to my own lack of expertise in Roman law, and the second relating to the scarcity, imprecision, and complex interpretation of antique sources treating this subject. That said, however, the preceding portrait does align with the Gospel accounts of Jesus'

---

16. See appendix 2 of the work by Jochen Bleicken, *Senatsgericht und Kaisergericht. Eine Studie zur Entwicklung des Prozessrechtes im frühen Prinzipat*, Abhandlungen der Akademie der Wissensschaften in Göttingen, phil.-hist. Klasse, 3. Folge, 54 (Göttingen: Vandenhoeck & Ruprecht, 1962), 166–88; as well as the articles suggested in the bibliography, which appeared in the *Revue internationale des droits de l'antiquité*, 3rd ser., 11 (1964).

17. See the First Cyrene Edict.

trial, allowing the following statement to be made with some confidence: Jesus was judged by the governor, in person, who represented the person of the emperor. His trial thus followed the procedure of the *cognitio extra ordinem*.

Under the *cognitio extra ordinem*, the governor, surrounded by advisers filling a merely consultative function, could organize and direct the proceedings at will. Enjoying a large margin of freedom, he could summon parties, hear the plaintiff's accusations, evaluate the punishability and guilt of the accused, issue the sentence, and fix the punishment without making reference even to specific laws. Apparently, the stages and categories of a trial, carefully distinguished under the *ordo*, could be disregarded and regrouped at will under the *cognitio extra ordinem*—and they were in the case of Jesus.

Though free in certain ways, the functionary judge did not enjoy complete freedom. Evidently, he still needed to respect the essential principles of the law. It was his duty to avoid judiciary errors and to protect the poor against the unjust persecution of the powerful. During the interrogation, the governor equally was obliged to give each party the floor and to seek to establish impartially his own opinion of the case. Furthermore, as representative of the emperor, he was obligated to respect all existing imperial *mandata*. Subject to the whims of the emperor and the recriminations of provincial officials, the governors frequently tended to have their opinions dictated to them by the emperor (evidence of this can be found, for instance, in the correspondence between Pliny the Younger and Trajan, where it appears that the emperor chafed at the lack of initiative in the governor of Bithynia).

Pilate, operating under the *extra ordinem* procedure, opened a veritable trial (*pro tribunali*) of Jesus' case, not merely an investigation (*de plano*). The mentions made in Matthew and John—albeit late in date—of the *bêma* (bench, seat) of the governor (Matt. 27:19; John 19:13) indicate this distinction clearly. As might be anticipated, Pilate first gave the floor to the *delatores*, the Jewish leaders who brought accusations against Jesus. For these accusations, they surely could not refer their complaints to a specific law. Instead, they referenced actions and attitudes universally blamable from a Roman perspective, like Jesus' disturbance of the public order and disobedience of the emperor by virtue of his messianic pretensions, both strongly political in nature.

Respectful of procedure, Pilate would next have given the floor to the accused. To the governor's surprise, Jesus employed none of the means criminals traditionally called on to move the judge (ragged hair, somber garments, imploring and submissive postures; see Josephus, *Jewish Antiquities* 14.9.4 §172). Instead, Jesus was silent. The Gospels depict Pilate's hesitation, faced with this silence, and his hesitation does not stretch verisimilitude. Some critics contend that Pilate's hesitation responds to early Christians' desire to exonerate Pilate more than it expresses his historical response. And it is true that the Synoptic Gospels tend to exculpate Pilate under an apologetic aim. In fact, their portrayal of the governor is quite at odds with portraits of the same offered by Philo and Josephus, who depict him as a cruel, unscrupulous character. But three different explanations could account for these discrepancies: one, Pilate may have aimed, by resisting the pressure of the Jewish authorities in Jesus' case, to prove his superiority and independence; two, the Gospels may whitewash Pilate here, as they tend to do, out of apologetic motives (freeing Pilate from blame allowed Christians to place the bulk of the responsibility for Jesus' death on their principal adversaries, the Jews); three, Pilate's attitude may have evolved over time, following developments in imperial political relations with Judaism. Whichever of these scenarios is correct, the fact remains that Pilate clearly did not wish to yield to the Jews on Jesus' case. While he may have feared the reaction of the crowd, he still did not feel inclined to bow to the Jewish leaders' designs. It is possible, therefore, that the behavior of the accused caught him sincerely off guard.

Luke reports that Pilate, after a brief interrogation, sent Jesus to Herod. Some critics have held that Pilate was required by law to enact this transfer. So Luke contends, "When Pilate heard this, he asked whether the man was a Galilean. And when he learned that he was under Herod's jurisdiction, he sent him off to Herod, who was himself in Jerusalem at that time" (Luke 23:6–7). A criminal, as the argument in favor of this episode's historicity runs, needed to be tried in his province of habitation (*forum domicilii*), not the province in which the crime was committed (*forum delicti*). But this procedure developed later and even then seems to have affected only the jurisdiction of the *ordo*. In the early days of the Principate, cases were tried in the province in which the crime was committed. The transfer to Herod would not, therefore, have been legally necessary. If anything, it would seem to have entailed rather a gesture of respect toward Herod or perhaps a holdover of the privilege exercised by Herod the Great to extradite criminals who had fled. In truth, Jesus the Galilean was punishable in Judea by the Roman governor. In any case, the historicity of Jesus' appearance before Herod is far from sure. The episode may correspond instead, as Acts 4:27 suggests, to the evangelist's desire to realize the words of the messianic Psalm 2: "The kings of the earth set themselves, and the rulers take counsel together, against the Lord and his anointed" (Ps 2:2). If this psalm did inspire the Herod episode, the episode is probably not historically authentic.[18]

Having said that, it is worth noting nevertheless that the *Gospel of Peter* also introduces Herod into the story's cast of characters. Although the fragmentary nature of the text makes it difficult to ascertain the part the Galilean ruler played in the narrative, the text does relate that Herod, unlike Pilate, but like the Jews and other judges, did not wash his hands of Jesus' blood. This statement implies the prince's guilt in the shedding of that blood. In fact, the text adds that Herod—whether by order from Pilate or not is unclear—arranged matters so that he himself could take charge of Jesus, to lead him to execution. Finally, the text also notes how Pilate, though willing to allow Joseph of Arimathea to collect Jesus' body after the crucifixion, curiously enough consults first with Herod before consenting. Whatever we make of these narrative details, it is clear that the *Gospel of Peter* shares with Luke the opinion that the Galilean ruler was in

18. Some historians have identified Herod as the *iudex datus* chosen by the governor. This hypothesis seems unlikely, however, since in Judea the governor would have judged capital trials himself.

Jerusalem during Jesus' trial and, moreover, that he was not unconnected to the fate of the accused. This presentation of Herod's role may in fact hold traces of remembered history. After all, it is quite possible that Herod would have left Galilee, where he ruled, to travel to Jerusalem, the Holy City, for the Passover celebration.

The next episode, that strange interlude concerning Barabbas, appears with greater or lesser detail in all the canonical Gospels (in addition to the Gospel accounts, see Acts 3:13–14). Apparently it was customary for the governor to free a single prisoner during the Passover, to satisfy the crowd. It would seem, from the Gospel narratives, that a crowd came forward during Pilate's trial of Jesus to "ask Pilate to do for them according to his custom" (Mark 15:8). The historicity of this Passover dispensation is debatable, since no other text confirms the custom.[19] Yet textual silence does not warrant divesting the episode of all historical merit. For there is no clear apologetic, scriptural, or legendary motive that would have inspired its creation. On the contrary, one element of the episode has long shocked Christians, a fact that rather argues for the historicity of the episode: the criminal's name is Jesus Barabbas. The discomfort this caused among Christians may be discerned from the fact that most manuscripts exclude the name Jesus, retaining only the name Barabbas to identify the other criminal. Finally, this episode alone—as mysterious and offensive to the principles of the most elementary justice as it may be—accounts for the presence of the crowd in the vicinity of the Praetorium.

Now, the high priests specifically wished to eliminate Jesus without stirring up the crowd. Evidently, they did not succeed, since the crowd arrived right in the midst of everything and

---

19. See Gordon Thomas, *The Trial: The Life and Inevitable Crucifixion of Jesus* (London: Bantam, 1987), 218–19. Thomas examines the practice of amnesty in Jewish and Roman law. In particular, he observes that the Romans distinguished between two types of pardon, *abolitio* (amnesty) and *indulgentia* (remission of a punishment). In his estimation, the Romans inherited from the Greeks the custom of pardoning in connection with large religious festivals.

demanded the release of a prisoner, according to custom. From that moment, the crowd became a player in the drama of Jesus' trial. The high priests undertook to provoke the crowd against Jesus of Nazareth. Did Pilate, on his side, attempt to consult the populace in making his judgment? The *vox populi* may have claimed some attention in the Orient of the first century, under the influence of Hellenistic law. Public opinion, for instance, would have clamored to recall to local magistrates in free cities their duties as representatives of the people. Yet it is inaccurate to imagine that the vociferous crowd, as if by some explicit vote, condemned Jesus to death.[20] The final decision had to come only from Pilate. It is accurate, however, to say that Pilate made his decision under pressure from the crowd. Jerusalem may not have been a free city, but still the governor could not remain indifferent to the outcry of the crowd. Yielding to that pressure, Pilate may have hoped to protect himself from further demands.[21]

In the end, Pilate condemned Jesus to death. The shock some have expressed at the Gospels' phrasing of Pilate's sentence—"After flogging Jesus, he handed him over to be crucified" (Mark 15:15)—proves misplaced. True, to the untrained eye, this phrase might not appear to relate a sentence at all. In fact, the line exactly sums up one possible end of a trial by *cognitio extra ordinem*. In an *extra ordinem* trial, as mentioned earlier, the judge had to determine at once the punishability, guilt, and punishment of the accused. This phrase from Mark 15:15 cites the punishment Pilate fixed, thereby implicitly confirming his determination of Jesus' punishability and his guilt. Roman

20. This is the argument put forward by Jean Colin, *Les villes libres de l'Orient gréco-romain et l'envoi au supplice par acclamations populaires* (Brussels: Latomus, Revue d'études latines, 1965).

21. Roman jurists were well aware that the crowd could exercise pressure on judges. For this reason, they prescribed that judges not allow themselves to be swayed by public opinion and the shouts of the crowd. The *Code of Justinian* 9.47.12 relates a text by Diocletian and Maximianus on this issue: "Vanae voces populi non sunt audiendae," "The vain voices of the people must not be attended"; see Bickermann, "Utilitas Crucis," 209–10.

jurists summarized in similar terms the concluding pronouncement of capital sentences in such trials: *duci iussit*, "he ordered
that he be led to execution."[22]

As was customary, Pilate had Jesus beaten with rods before his
crucifixion (Roman jurists distinguished between the light beating, *fustigatio*, issued as a deterring punishment [see Luke 23:16]
and the *flagellatio* that normally preceded crucifixion).[23] The
Roman soldiers, for their part, transformed this customary beating into a grotesque scene staged for their own amusement. No
doubt imitating a carnival or circus game—the model for such
games is attested to by several ancient texts[24]—they made Jesus'
punishment into their merriment. Like the "king" chosen by lot
in Roman festivals of Saturnalia, Jesus received all the emblems
of royalty (thence the purple tunic, the reed, the crown of
thorns). Evidently the Roman soldiers did not mean by this allusion to celebrate the Roman festival; rather, parodying a parody,
they took up this sort of play to divert themselves.

This scene complete, Jesus was charged with his cross. He
would have carried only the transverse portion of the cross, the
patibulum, as the vertical post would have been fixed already in the
ground. Weakened with beating and faint from exertion, Jesus fal-
tered on the way to Golgotha. To assist him, the soldiers sum-
moned a man named Simon, originally from Cyrenaica. This
man, who was returning from the fields, carried Jesus' cross the
rest of the way (Mark 15:21). According to Mark 15:23 and
Matthew 27:34, someone then offered Jesus wine mixed with
myrrh, which he refused.[25] Rabbinic tradition teaches that this

22. A trial by *ordo* would conclude differently. The jury would give its verdict of
innocence or guilt. Then the law regarding the particular crime of which the accused
was held guilty would indicate the corresponding punishment to the magistrate.

23. See Titus Livy, *The History of Rome from Its Foundation* 33.36.3.

24. Philo, *In Flaccum* 6.36–39; Martial, *De spectaculis* 7; *Martyre de saint Dasius*, ed.
Franz Cumont, *Analecta Bollandiana* 16 (1897): 5–16.

25. Matt. 27:48, Mark 15:36, and Luke 23:36 also mention that, later, on the cross,
Jesus was offered a sponge soaked in vinegar. John 19:28–30 affirms the same fact,
advancing further that Jesus, who had first expressed his desire for it by those famous
words "I am thirsty," took the drink.

intoxicating beverage, meant to stupefy the condemned and lessen their suffering, was prepared by pious women from the city.[26]

And then, as the Gospels say with unparalleled brevity, "They crucified him" (Mark 15:24). Just over thirty years ago, archaeologists discovered the remains of a crucified man in an ossuary in Jerusalem.[27] This discovery has allowed for a more precise understanding of the way in which the body was hung on the cross. This particular man had been affixed with three nails, one in each forearm and a long one through the linked heels. The legs were pressed together, with the knees bent. A wooden support, placed under the buttocks, prevented the flesh from tearing and the body from thereby falling free. In so doing, the support merely prolonged the agony. This agony could endure for hours, as the crucified ceaselessly strove to hold himself upright, thus fighting against the asphyxiation and tetanus that would bring death. Jesus' death was relatively quick, quick enough, in fact, to elicit remark from Pilate (Mark 15:44). Most modern physicians hold that Jesus died from cardiac arrest, brought on by progressive asphyxiation. The report in the Synoptic Gospels, that Jesus gave forth a loud cry before dying, astonishes, since the crucified perish slowly by suffocation.

The seven words Jesus speaks from the cross derive from the exegetical agendas and legendary developments of each evangelist, not from history. The first saying appears in Mark and Matthew, the only saying uttered by the crucified Jesus in these Gospels: "'*Eloi, Eloi, lema sabachthani?*' which means, 'My God, my God, why have you forsaken me?'" (Mark 15:34 and Matt. 27:46; Mark's version is quoted here).[28] No doubt this saying was attributed to Jesus *a posteriori*, as Jesus came to represent for early Christians the model of the just man who unjustly suffers. Moreover, Psalm 22, whose second verse is quoted here in both Aramaic and

---

26. See Babylonian Talmud, *Sanhedrin* 6 or, by another demarcation of the text, 43a.

27. See the articles published in *Israel Exploration Journal* 20 (1970), indicated in the bibliography.

28. As mentioned above, the *Gospel of Peter* transmits a particular version of this same saying by the distraught Jesus: "My power, O power, thou hast forsaken me" (*Gos. Pet.* 19).

Greek, belongs to the literary genre of individual prayers for rescue. In recounting this saying, the tradition depicts Jesus paradoxically as a pious Jew who feels tragically abandoned by God.

Three further words flow from the pen of the evangelist Luke. The first reads, "Father, forgive them; for they do not know what they are doing" (Luke 23:34).[29] The wish to exonerate the judges who condemned Jesus, as this saying aims to do, corresponds with Luke's larger theology. The evangelist will reiterate this same request for forgiveness in Acts, placing it on the lips of Stephen, the first Christian martyr, whose lot parallels that of his Lord (Acts 7:60). The second Lukan saying comes in Jesus' response to the repentant thief: "Truly I tell you, today you will be with me in Paradise" (23:43). The thieves, receiving only a discrete mention in Mark (Mark 15:27), attract more notice in Luke's Gospel, as well as in the *Gospel of Peter*.[30] Here then is the third word that Jesus speaks from the cross in Luke's Gospel: "Father, into your hands I commend my spirit" (23:46). Like the first Lukan word, this final word signals the endurance of Jesus' faith even unto the instant of his cruel and unjust death. As with the first word, the evangelist— or the tradition he follows—here strengthens the proof of Jesus' faith by placing on Jesus' lips as he dies words from the Psalms (in this case Ps. 31:6, though the evangelist adds the invocation to the "Father," missing from the psalm).

The final three words from the cross come from the Gospel of John. In the first, Jesus addresses Mary and the beloved disciple, conversing together: "When Jesus saw his mother and the disciple whom he loved standing beside her, he said to his mother, 'Woman, here is your son.' Then he said to the disciple, 'Here is

---

29. I understand this prayer to belong to the ancient layer of the Third Gospel, even if several of the most ancient manuscripts do not include it. If some manuscripts omit it, this omission is surely because, in the eyes of the copyists, those who killed Jesus—far from being pardoned by God—had already been punished. According to these scribes, the fall of Jerusalem offered proof of God's judgment.

30. The *Gospel of Peter* also introduces the two malefactors, placing on the lips of one the following words of reproach to those who divide the Lord's garments: "We have landed in suffering for the deeds of wickedness which we have committed, but this man, who has become the saviour of men, what wrong has he done you?" (*Gos. Pet.* 13).

your mother.' And from that hour the disciple took her into his own home" (19:26–27). This double provision, of a son to a mother and a mother to a son, reveals more of Johannine theology than it does of historical reality. The evangelist sees and expresses that new relationships form at the foot of the cross, binding together an ecclesial community in which the biological family must give way to the spiritual family. From a historical point of view, it seems that Matthew and Mark portray the crucifixion scene more accurately when they show the disciples to have fled and hidden themselves in their distress at such a disaster (Mark 14:50 and Matt. 26:56).[31] The Johannine Jesus' second word, mentioned earlier, suggests all the suffering of those last moments, as Jesus cries out, "I am thirsty" (19:28), before receiving the sponge of vinegar. Finally, John's Gospel records one last saying from the cross. At the moment of death, the Christ proclaims, "It is finished" (19:30). This word, like the others, manifests John's theology: however revolting and absurd Jesus' death may seem, it brings about the accomplishment of God's plan. This fulfillment comes with the arrival of the Johannine Jesus' long-awaited "hour" on the cross (see John 2:4; 7:30; 8:20; 12:23, 27; 13:1; 17:1).

A glance back through these seven sayings from the cross confirms that they do not belong to the category of history. Instead, they reveal scriptural and theological reflection or legendary narrative details, like those that will fill the narratives of later Christian martyrs. The words Jesus spoke from the cross, if indeed he spoke, do not appear in the Gospel narratives.

What happened to Jesus' disciples, friends, and family during these dark hours? As mentioned earlier, the evangelists do not agree on this subject. Mark and Matthew, who depict the disciples' flight, seem to stay closer to historical truth than Luke and John. If the fourth evangelist places the beloved disciple at the foot of the cross, he does so to prove the continuing process of revelation, from God to Christ and from Christ to his beloved disciple (the one who reclined, at the Last Supper, upon Jesus' breast [John 13:23, 25], just as the Son is held close to the heart of the Father [John 1:18]). As

31. I will address Luke's perspective on this question (Luke 23:49) below.

for the third evangelist, who wishes to preserve the disciples' repu-tation, he contents himself with saying merely that they stood off at a distance (Luke 23:49). In this discreet way, he admits that the dis-ciples were not near to Jesus in his agony. Yet his embarrassment is clear in that he avoids using his habitual terms "disciples," "apos-tles," or "the Twelve" (or, rather, the Eleven) in this verse, but speaks vaguely instead of Jesus' "acquaintances." On this question of the disciples' presence or absence at the cross, then, Mark's and Matthew's testimonies must be trusted; both Gospels affirm that all the disciples fled (Mark 14:50; Matt. 26:56). At first, the disciples surely holed up somewhere in Jerusalem or the surrounding area. Later they returned to Galilee. The *Gospel of Peter* confirms this view: "But I mourned with my fellows, and being wounded in heart we hid ourselves, for we were sought after by them as evildoers and as persons who wanted to set fire to the Temple" (*Gos. Pet.* 26). This last element, absent from the canonical accounts, doubtless repre-sents another legendary development, for it extends to the disciples the threat of the Temple's destruction attributed to Jesus in his life. While it is not impossible that Jesus' family—particularly Mary, his mother, and James, his brother—were in Jerusalem for the Passover celebration, the testimony of John 19:26–27 does not suffice for placing Mary historically at the foot of the cross.

The crucifixion complete, Jesus was buried. Simple enough, it would seem, but even the question of Jesus' burial raises complex questions. In Palestine, the corpses of the executed were usually placed in common tombs located near the execution sites, but dis-tinct from other cemeteries. It was not permissible for the impurity of the executed to contaminate the remains of more upstanding people (see Deut. 21:22–23).[32] The Jews, however, took care that even those condemned to death received decent burials, for if a

---

32. This impurity lasted as long as the flesh was not completely decomposed (Mishnah, *Sanhedrin* 6.6 or, by another demarcation of the text, 6.8). After that point, the bones could be collected and placed in the family ossuary. This was precisely the case with the crucified man whose skeleton was recently discovered in Jerusalem. Traces of ointment on the bones, applied at the moment of the transfer, indicate that this man's family sought to complete the traditional rights due to the departed one whom they continued to honor.

body was "left without its portion of earth," it would thereby receive "more than its just penalty."[33]

All the Gospels, including the *Gospel of Peter*, agree that Jesus' body was not placed in the common tomb reserved for the executed, but in a private tomb. Joseph of Arimathea, one of Jesus' admirers, seems to have been behind this exception.[34] He requested Pilate's permission to take Jesus' body; Pilate assented and gave it to him. The Gospels then report that Joseph laid Jesus in his own tomb. The unanimity of the sources on this point must not, however, lull us into blind acceptance. After all, a private tomb, and an easily locatable one, is essential to the Christian apologia. Without a tomb, the narrative of the empty tomb cannot stand. Interestingly enough, however, the Jews never seem to have evoked the problem of a common tomb's anonymity in their anti-Christian polemics. They did insinuate that Jesus' body was stolen away (Matt. 28:13–15; *Gos. Pet.* 30–33), but this insinuation, too, implies beyond a doubt that he lay in a private, particular tomb. The support for the historicity of the Joseph of Arimathea episode grows. One final text, however, and a contrary one, demands our notice: Acts 13:27–29, which seems to derive from a more ancient, less legendary tradition than the Gospels, relates that Jesus was buried by the very Jews who accused him, evidently, in the common tomb.

33. Josephus, *Jewish Antiquities* 4.8.24 §265, trans. H. Thackeray (Cambridge, MA: Harvard University Press, 1967).

34. Matt. 27:60 and John 19:41 assert that Joseph of Arimathea placed Jesus' body in a new tomb, located in a garden. The *Gospel of Peter* gives the following report: "And the Jews rejoiced and gave his body to Joseph that he might bury it, since he had seen all the good that he [= Jesus] had done. And he took the Lord, washed him, wrapped him in linen and brought him into his own sepulchre, called Joseph's Garden" (*Gos. Pet.* 23–24).

Chapter Four

Times and Places

The attempt to situate the places of the passion and the chronology of Holy Week raises subtle difficulties for the historian. The upper room, Gethsemane, the high priest's house, the room where the Sanhedrin met, Pilate's praetorium, Golgotha, the Holy Sepulchre—not one of these places can be located with any certainty. Since the archaeological complexities of each of these locations are too dense to detail here, suffice it to say that Gethsemane, which probably means "olive press," must have been found on the east side of the Kidron valley, either at the foot or on the slopes of the Mount of Olives. On the normal location of the Sanhedrin's meeting place, the Mishnah, the Talmud, and Josephus do not agree. The New Testament accounts further complicate this question, as they do not divulge whether the Sanhedrin met for Jesus' trial in its habitual place or in the high priest's palace. As for Pilate, the sources situate him at "a place called The Stone Pavement [*Lithostrotos*], or in Hebrew Gabbatha" (John 19:13).[1] But they do not specify whether this place was at the Antonia fortress at the northwest corner of the Temple precincts, or at Herod's palace, to the west of the city. Even the word "praetorium" (Matt. 27:27) does not necessarily refer to a fixed site, since the ancients

1. The Greek word *Lithostrotos* designates a place paved with stones, a pavement.

may have used it to refer to any place where the governor chose to hold a tribunal. Golgotha, apparently a place shaped like a skull, and the tomb in which Jesus was laid must have been situated close to each other, perhaps near those places within the bounds of the Church of the Holy Sepulchre that pilgrims venerate today. Hadrian, the Roman emperor, did historians a great service in settling at this spot the forum of *Aelia capitolina* (namely, pagan Jerusalem reconstructed in the second century CE) and building on it a temple to Aphrodite. His polemical action suggests that this spot housed another holy place, itself venerated in the first century, surely in this case the Holy Sepulchre.[2]

The chronology of the passion proves equally difficult to establish. The canonical Gospels unanimously attest that Jesus died on a Friday, on the eve of the Sabbath (see Mark 15:42 and John 19:31). In the Gospel of John, this same day was also the day of preparation for the Passover, Nisan 14. For, according to John, the Passover fell that year on the Sabbath (see John 19:31). By this dating, John aligns Jesus' death with the hour at which the Passover lambs were being slaughtered in the Temple. His wish to identify Jesus as the paschal lamb of the new covenant (John 1:29, 36; 19:36) may well have determined this symbolic chronology. Mark, on the other hand, paints Jesus' last meal as a paschal meal; his dating places Jesus' death on the very day of the Passover, Nisan 15. Yet this chronology, with its own typological aims, also raises difficulties: could the Sanhedrin have met on the day of the Passover? Does not Mark himself admit that the Jewish leaders wished to avoid executing Jesus during the high festival (Mark 14:2)? The awkward phrase "On the first day of Unleavened Bread, when the Passover lamb is sacrificed" (Mark 14:12) may indicate that Mark was but poorly acquainted with the Jewish calendar.[3]

---

2. See Eusebius of Caesarea, *Life of Constantine* 3.25–28; Clarendon Ancient History Series, trans. Averil Cameron and Stuart G. Hall (Oxford: Clarendon, 1999), 132–33 (translation) and 273–81 (commentary).

3. The sacrifice of the lambs occurred on the day of preparation for the feast, in this

Choosing the date of Jesus' death thus remains problematic, for the choice lies between John, who claims Nisan 14 for theological reasons, and Mark, who seems poorly informed with regard to Jewish practices. Even invoking the two different calendars in use at this time, the orthodox lunar calendar and the heterodox solar calendar, does not resolve all the difficulties that linger in the biblical testimony. One possible harmonization holds that Mark dated the new day from the rising of the sun, while John, following the Jewish authorities, dated it from sundown.

The time frame of Jesus' last day also varies from Gospel to Gospel. Mark spaces the day's events at three-hour intervals (see Mark 14:72; 15:1, 25, 33, 34, 42). This pattern seems too regular to be historically accurate. And John confirms only two moments in Mark's time frame: Peter's denial before the crowing of the cock (Mark 14:72; John 18:27) and Jesus' transfer to Pilate early in the morning at the first hour, that is, around six o'clock (Mark 15:1; John 18:28). But while Mark shows that Jesus is crucified at the third hour, around nine o'clock (Mark 15:25), John does not have Pilate hand Jesus over for crucifixion until the sixth hour, near noon (John 19:14). The *Gospel of Peter* confirms John's time frame: there, Jesus is crucified at noon (*Gos. Pet.* 15). This Gospel offers one further chronological precision. Like Mark (Mark 15:33), it indicates that an eclipse darkened the earth from the sixth to the ninth hour, that is, from noon to three o'clock. The *Gospel of Peter* goes further than Mark, however, in specifying that the deposition from the cross occurred at this time, at three o'clock. The closest we can come to a chronology is to suggest that Jesus was crucified around noon, died in the midafternoon, and was buried before sunset.

Only a few indications in the New Testament locate Jesus' ministry in history. By bringing these together, historians can affirm

---

case the eve of the Passover, Nisan 14. Leviticus 23:6 places the first day of unleavened bread on Nisan 15, also the date of the Passover. This complication can be reconciled only if Mark dates the beginning of the day with the dawn. The sacrifice would then fall in the afternoon, and the Passover meal, in the evening, on the same day. But this scenario does not seem realistic.

that Jesus died between 28 and 32 CE. If we follow John's chronology, he died on a Friday, Nisan 14. In this case, the Jewish lunar calendar yields two possible dates for Jesus' death: Friday, April 7, in the year 30 CE, or Friday, April 3, in the year 33 CE.[4]

4. In treating this delicate question, in which I am no specialist, I have relied on Jack Finegan's manual, *Handbook of Biblical Chronology: Principles of Time Reckoning in the Ancient World and Problems of Chronology in the Bible* (Princeton, NJ: Princeton University Press, 1964), 285–98, and the summary provided in the article "Zeitrechnung" by Alfred Jepsen and August Strobel in *Biblisch-Historisches Handwörterbuch*, ed. Bo Reicke and Leonhard Rost, vol. 3 (Göttingen: Vandenhoeck & Ruprecht, 1966), cols. 2211–28.

Chapter Five

Conclusion

No witness to Jesus' passion watched every event. From the outset, anyone who wished to relate its incidents needed also to rely on the accounts of other witnesses. Furthermore, no witness watched the passion events unmediated. What each witness saw passed through the lenses of consciousness and language, themselves vehicles of interpretation. The reconstructions of the passion drama in the mind of a high priest, a Roman soldier, and a disciple would thus necessarily differ. One of the Jewish leaders might have emphasized the role played by the Sanhedrin, might have remembered Jesus as a false prophet. Pilate, on the other hand, probably knew nothing of Jesus' previous appearance before the Jewish high priest, probably saw in Jesus a political agitator. The disciples in their turn knew that Jesus had faced the Jewish, then the Roman, authorities, but did they follow the legal subtleties that directed his fate? Or did they not swell the responsibility of the Jews while lessening that of Pilate? It seems they did. They also admit to have despaired, fled, and even denied the one they followed. Might they not exaggerate, to emphasize God's power in transforming the situation at Easter? In fact, it's possible. In any case, their understanding of Jesus would change utterly with Easter. Until that moment, they knew they were drawn to Jesus and they affirmed that he came from God, but they barely understood what that meant.

One common denominator links all the participants in the passion drama: they all knew that the Jews had arrested Jesus and denounced him to Pilate. They also knew that Pilate, under public pressure, had condemned and executed him. This common understanding seems almost schematic in its simplicity. It addresses neither the aims of the accused, the stakes of the trial, nor the result of the drama, the resurrection. On these points, the historian must enter into conversation with the Christian theologian, who identifies the eruption of a new era, the shift from an old to a new economy with the resurrection, a historically unprovable event.

If the resurrection, taken in itself, escapes the bounds of time and, consequently, history, it nevertheless remains linked to the spatio-temporal framework in which it emerged. According to the accounts of the first witnesses, the resurrection communicates the bestowal of divine power on Jesus, showing him openly to be the Messiah. The title "Messiah," in Greek, "Christ," assumes from that moment full force; it shakes loose any previous ambiguity or reserve. The title "Lord" similarly aims to signify, both in Aramaic and Greek, the imperial power of the Risen One. An archaic formula, preserved in the speech that Luke attributes to Peter on the day of Pentecost, articulates this transformation: "God has made him both Lord and Messiah, this Jesus whom you crucified" (Acts 2:36). The most ancient witnesses further celebrate the new power given to Christ through a recurring motif of exaltation, of lifting up: "This Jesus God raised up, and of that all of us are witnesses. Being therefore exalted at the right hand of God, and having received from the Father the promise of the Holy Spirit, he has poured out this that you both see and hear" (Acts 2:32–33).

From the very start, the first Christians turned to the Scriptures of Israel for a confirmation of their new faith and an explanation of their paschal message. They surely rejoiced in finding and applying to Jesus Christ the first verse of Psalm 110 (109), "The LORD says to my lord, 'Sit at my right hand until I make your enemies your footstool.'" They also made use of the book of Daniel, with its description of the Son of Man. Daniel 7:13–14 allowed them to prove scripturally the new power conferred on Christ, as well as to announce his next coming: "As I watched in the night visions, I saw one like a Son of Man coming with the clouds of heaven. And he came to the Ancient One and was presented before him. To him was given dominion and glory and kingship, that all peoples, nations, and languages should serve him."

When the first Christians had to prove the truth and value of their new faith they sought proof in the Scriptures, on the one hand, and, on the other, in the accounts of witnesses to the resurrection appearances. Names of specific disciples were put forth, especially Mary Magdalene, Peter, and James. Lists of these eyewitnesses were even drawn up. Paul preserves such a list, one appended by his memories and his personal experience:

> For I handed on to you as of first importance what I in turn had received: that Christ died for our sins in accordance with the scriptures, and that he was buried, and that he was raised on the third day in accordance with the scriptures, and that he appeared to Cephas, then to the twelve. Then he appeared to more than five hundred brothers and sisters at one time, most of whom are still alive, though some have died. Then he appeared to James, then to all the apostles. Last of all, as to one untimely born, he appeared also to me. (1 Cor. 15:3–8)

The appearance to Cephas, the Semitic equivalent for "Peter," finds confirmation in an allusion made at the close of the Lukan episode of the disciples on the road to Emmaus: the Eleven affirm to Cleophas and his friend, "The Lord has risen indeed, and he has appeared to Simon!" (Luke 24:34; Simon being the one whose surname is Cephas, in Aramaic, and Peter, in Greek). The appearance to James, without a doubt the brother of the Lord and not the son of Zebedee, is also attested to by the author of a Judeo-Christian Gospel, *The Gospel of the Hebrews*:

"And when the Lord had given the linen cloth to the servant of the priest, he went to James and appeared to him."[1] For reasons that may be divined, the appearance of the Risen One to Mary of Magdala, that is to say, Mary Magdalene, does not figure in Paul's list of eyewitnesses to the resurrection (1 Cor. 15:3–8). Since Jewish law did not recognize the testimony of women, Mary Magdalene's account would have been undesirable to certain eyes, as it would actually have diminished, not bolstered, the weight of proof in the list. Moreover, competition existed from the start between the diverse Christian groups; it may be that Paul did not recognize the ecclesial community built on Mary Magdalene's testimony. Though absent from Paul's list, the appearance to Mary Magdalene does occur in two Gospel narratives, John 20:11–18 and Matthew 28:9–10 (in the latter case, "the other Mary" accompanies Mary Magdalene). The verses commonly called the inauthentic end of Mark—added to the Second Gospel over the course of the second century—also attest to the appearance to Mary Magdalene: "Now after he rose early on the first day of the week, he appeared first to Mary Magdalene, from whom he had cast out seven demons. She went out and told those who had been with him, while they were mourning and weeping. But when they heard that he was alive and had been seen by her, they would not believe it" (Mark 16:9–11).

New Testament exegetes frequently distinguish between two types of Easter narratives: between appearance stories and empty-tomb stories. In the first type, the resurrected Christ appears to an individual or a group, showing himself to be fully alive. Often the witnesses to the appearance have difficulty recognizing the Risen One, a fact that attests to the new quality of life the Crucified now manifests. His resurrection passes beyond the resuscitation of Lazarus, for Jesus does more than merely recuperate his lost vitality. He actually recovers his divine iden-

---

1. Jerome preserves this fragment in his *De viris illustribus* 2 (Patrologia latina 23, cols. 642–43). The translation cited here comes from *New Testament Apocrypha*, ed. Wilhelm Schneemelcher, rev. ed. (Louisville, KY: Westminster/John Knox Press, 1991), 178.

tity, an identity now tinged by the particular experiences of his incarnation and passion. He is evidently so transformed that Mary Magdalene originally mistakes him for the gardener (John 20:15). The disciples also struggle to recognize him during their encounter on the lake shore (John 21:4–7). In the Emmaus episode too, it takes the breaking of the bread for the two disciples' eyes to be opened to his identity (Luke 24:30-31).[2] In the Gospel of John as well, narrative details depict the qualitatively new identity of the Risen One. A locked room on an upper floor poses no difficulty to the Johannine Christ, who enters mysteriously into the midst of those gathered there (John 20:19, 26). Lest such behavior lead some to confuse these appearances with those of a ghost, the Lukan Christ proposes to eat in the disciples' presence and shares a morsel of grilled fish with them (Luke 24:41–43).

If the stories in which the Risen One appears to an individual serve the specific functions of attesting to the resurrection and depicting the moment of recognition, thereby proving the continuity between the earthly Jesus and the celestial Christ, the appearances to a group of disciples serve a further purpose: they justify the missionary enterprise and serve as an argument for ecclesiastical development. In Matthew, the risen Christ commissions the Eleven, who have gathered on a mountain, to go forth and evangelize all the earth (Matt. 28:16–20). Similarly, in Luke, Jesus comforts these same Eleven by explaining to them the greater divine plan: through his ministry, passion, and resurrection, Jesus teaches them, he has fulfilled the Scriptures. He proclaims to the disciples gathered around him the impending descent of the Spirit at Pentecost and he designates them as witnesses and missionaries, called to proclaim Jesus' resurrection and the coming of the kingdom of God

---

2. A passage from the inauthentic end to the Gospel of Mark summarizes the Emmaus episode in the following manner: "After this he appeared in another form to two of them, as they were walking into the country. And they went back and told the rest, but they did not believe them" (Mark 16:12–13). As this brief reprisal corresponds but imperfectly to the Lukan account, many exegetes hold that the author of the inauthentic ending to Mark relied on oral tradition for this episode, rather than Luke 24:13–35.

(Luke 24:36–49 and John 20:21–23).[3] The inauthentic ending of Mark narrates a similar appearance to the Eleven, seemingly combining the accounts found in Matthew and Luke:

> Later he appeared to the eleven themselves as they were sitting at the table; and he upbraided them for their lack of faith and stubbornness, because they had not believed those who saw him after he had risen. And he said to them, "Go into all the world and proclaim the good news to the whole creation. The one who believes and is baptized will be saved; but the one who does not believe will be condemned. And these signs will accompany those who believe: by using my name they will cast out demons; they will speak in new tongues; they will pick up snakes in their hands, and if they drink any deadly thing, it will not hurt them; they will lay their hands on the sick, and they will recover." (Mark 16:14–18)

The *Gospel of Peter* breaks off suddenly at the beginning of a scene that must have read much like John 21:1–14, a resurrection appearance on the shores of Lake Gennesaret: "Now it was the last day of unleavened bread and many went away and repaired to their homes, since the feast was at an end. But we, the twelve disciples of the Lord, wept and mourned, and each one, very grieved for what had come to pass, went to his own home. But I, Simon Peter, and my brother Andrew took our nets and went off to the sea. And there was with us Levi, the son of Alphaeus, whom the Lord . . ." (*Gos. Pet.* 58–60).

The second type of resurrection story centers on the discovery of the empty tomb. A group of visitors, most often women, arrives

---

3. In the Acts of the Apostles, Luke narrates the fulfillment of this promised Spirit's descent (Acts 2:1–13) and goes on to show how the disciples fulfill their duty as witnesses (2:32; 3:15; 5:32; 10:40–42). To announce Jesus' resurrection (Acts 2:24, for example) means at once to proclaim the kingdom of God (see Acts 28:31, Paul's final proclamation), to recount Jesus' whole life and ministry (see Acts 10:37–41), and to foretell the return of the Son and the final judgment (see, for example, Acts 10:42 and 17:31).

at the tomb the morning after the Sabbath, at the earliest moment when work and journeys are again permitted. They do not intend to encounter one living, but to venerate one dead. Thus they come bearing perfumes and aromatic ointments, prepared to practice the customary mourning of their religion. According to the Gospel narratives, the *Gospel of Peter* included, they arrive to find the stone rolled away and an empty tomb. One or two heavenly messengers populate the scene, to meet their perplexity with an explanation. The core of this explanation touches on the divine victory over death in Jesus, who is absent because he has been resurrected. Such an empty-tomb story closes the primitive version of the Gospel of Mark, in which no resurrection appearance follows (Mark 16:1–8). The Gospels of Matthew and Luke also take up this scene (Matt. 28:1–9 and Luke 24:1–10), and the *Gospel of Peter* likewise recounts a similar episode (*Gos. Pet.* 50–57).

It has been suggested that the origin of the appearance stories lies with male disciples, while the empty-tomb stories have their origin in female followers. Such a supposition does not attribute due weight to two related traditions, one centering on Mary Magdalene, the other on Peter. The appearance of the Risen One to Mary Magdalene cannot be considered a late legendary addition, nor does the story of Peter's visit to the empty tomb lack historical support. Both Matthew and John assert the appearance of the resurrected Christ to Mary Magdalene (Matt. 28:9–10 and John 20:11–18), while Luke and John both narrate Peter's visit to the empty tomb (Luke 24:12 and John 20:3–10, where the beloved disciple accompanies Peter in his visit).

Geographically speaking, the locations of the resurrection appearances remain enigmatic. Matthew recounts that the disciples returned to Galilee, to a particular mountain (Matt. 28:16). By the mention of this mountain, he means to recall the Sermon on the Mount (Matt. 5:1), an allusion that locates the mountain in Galilee. The last chapter of the Gospel of John[4] and the *Gospel*

---

4. Most biblical critics agree that the last chapter of John's Gospel is an addition, one that modifies the theological perspective of the rest of the Gospel by adding an imminently ecclesiological preoccupation.

of Peter similarly presuppose a Galilean location for the lakeside appearances they narrate (John 21:1–14 and *Gos. Pet.* 60). Conversely, Luke confines the disciples to Jerusalem, where they await the Pentecost and the irruption of the Spirit. The third evangelist specifies that Emmaus, where one resurrection appearance occurs, stands but a two-hour walk from Jerusalem (Luke 24:13), and that the Eleven reunite later that same day in Jerusalem (Luke 24:33). In this Gospel, Jesus finally leads his disciples to Bethany on the day of the ascension (Luke 24:50), and the disciples return again to Jerusalem after the final departure of their master (Luke 24:52). Since Luke evidently aims to endow the holy city with a pivotal function (probably under the influence of the oracle of Isa. 2:2–4), his placement of the resurrection appearances in Jerusalem must be understood to answer his theological goals. Most likely, the disciples, recognized elsewhere as Galileans by their accents (Matt. 26:73), returned home at that first moment of flight. The message of the resurrection must have reached them in their country and astonished them. It is possible that, in their enthusiasm over the Easter revelation, they decided to return to Jerusalem after the fact and wait there. What did they await? They probably waited for the return of the Son of Man, a return they expected imminently, perhaps even on the Jewish day of Pentecost. They joyously welcomed the coming of the Holy Spirit, for with it they anticipated the beginning of the Parousia. Other resurrection appearances probably arose in the capital during this initial period of euphoria and ecstatic beginnings. Realistic Paul aimed, in fact, to impose an end point to this initial series of appearances. Had he already realized the dubious profit to which Christians would turn that period between Easter and the ascension? Numerous Christian apocalypses (including the *Apocalypse of Peter*), as well as several dialogues with the Savior found at Nag Hammadi, reveal to modern readers how early Christians availed themselves of that period when the Risen One was present among his followers: by constructing long dialogues with the Risen One or scribing new revelations of the celestial Christ, ancient Christians could gain support for their own religious theories. While the resulting texts prove instructive on the Christian faith of the first centuries, they cannot help to reconstruct the last days of the Incarnate One and the first days of the Risen One.[5]

5. Readers can find the *Apocalypse of Peter*, the *Epistle of the Apostles*, and other texts depicting the disciples' conversations with the Risen One in *New Testament Apocrypha*, ed. Wilhelm Schneemelcher, rev. ed. 2 vols. (Louisville, KY: Westminster/John Knox Press, 1991). For the dialogues with the Risen One preserved in manuscripts from Nag Hammadi, see the English translation published under James M. Robinson's direction, *The Nag Hammadi Library in English, Translated and Introduced by Members of the Coptic Gnostic Library Project of the Institute for Antiquity and Christianity, Claremont, California*, with an afterword by Richard Smith (San Francisco: Harper Collins, 1988); see also the thirty volumes of the Bibliothèque copte de Nag Hammadi released to date in the "Textes" series of the Presses de l'Université Laval (Québec).

Appendixes

Luke 22:1–24:53[*]

The Plot against Jesus

22 Now the festival of Unleavened Bread, which is called the Passover, was near. [2] The chief priests and the scribes were looking for a way to put Jesus to death, for they were afraid of the people. [3] Then Satan entered into Judas called Iscariot, who was one of the twelve; [4] he went away and conferred with the chief priests and officers of the temple police about how he might betray him to them. [5] They were greatly pleased and agreed to give him money. [6] So he consented and began to look for an opportunity to betray him to them when no crowd was present.

The Preparation of the Passover

[7] Then came the day of Unleavened Bread, on which the Passover lamb had to be sacrificed. [8] So Jesus sent Peter and John, saying, "Go and prepare the Passover meal for us that we may eat it." [9] They asked him, "Where do you want us to make preparations for it?" [10] "Listen," he said to them, "when you have entered the city, a man carrying a jar of water will meet you; follow him into the house he enters [11] and say to the owner of the house, 'The teacher asks you, "Where is the guest room, where I may eat the Passover with my disciples?"' [12] He will show you a large room upstairs, already furnished. Make preparations for us

---

[*] The translation cited here, as elsewhere, is the *New Revised Standard Version.*

there." [13] So they went and found everything as he had told them; and they prepared the Passover meal.

The Last Supper

[14] When the hour came, he took his place at the table, and the apostles with him. [15] He said to them, "I have eagerly desired to eat this Passover with you before I suffer; [16] for I tell you, I will not eat it until it is fulfilled in the kingdom of God." [17] Then he took a cup, and after giving thanks he said, "Take this and divide it among yourselves; [18] for I tell you that from now on I will not drink of the fruit of the vine until the kingdom of God comes." [19] Then he took a loaf of bread, and when he had given thanks, he broke it and gave it to them, saying, "This is my body, which is given for you. Do this in remembrance of me." [20] And he did the same with the cup after supper, saying, "This cup that is poured out for you is the new covenant in my blood.

Announcement of the Betrayal

[21] "But see, the one who betrays me is with me, and his hand is on the table. [22] For the Son of Man is going as it has been determined, but woe to that one by whom he is betrayed!" [23] Then they began to ask one another which one of them it could be who would do this.

Warnings and Promises to the Twelve

[24] A dispute also arose among them as to which one of them was to be regarded as the greatest. [25] But he said to them, "The kings of the Gentiles lord it over them; and those in authority over them are called benefactors. [26] But not so with you; rather the greatest among you must become like the youngest, and the leader like one who serves. [27] For who is greater, the one who is at the table or the one who serves? Is it not the one at the table? But I am among you as one who serves. [28] You are those who have stood by me in my trials; [29] and I confer on you, just as my Father has conferred on me, a kingdom, [30] so that you may eat and drink at my table in my kingdom, and you will sit on thrones judging the twelve tribes of Israel."

Prediction of Peter's Denial

[31] "Simon, Simon, listen! Satan has demanded to sift all of you like wheat, [32] but I have prayed for you that your own faith may not fail; and you, when once you have turned back, strengthen your brothers." [33] And he said to him, "Lord, I am ready to go with you to prison and to death!" [34] Jesus said, "I tell you, Peter, the cock will not crow this day, until you have denied three times that you know me."

Imminence of the Ordeal

[35] He said to them, "When I sent you out without a purse, bag, or sandals, did you lack anything?" They said, "No, not a thing." [36] He said to them, "But now, the one who has a purse must take it, and likewise a bag. And the one who has no sword must sell his cloak and buy one. [37] For I tell you, this scripture must be fulfilled in me, 'And he was counted among the lawless'; and indeed what is written about me is being fulfilled." [38] They said, "Lord, look, here are two swords." He replied, "It is enough."

Prayer on the Mount of Olives

[39] He came out and went, as was his custom, to the Mount of Olives; and the disciples followed him. [40] When he reached the place, he said to them, "Pray that you may not come into the time of trial." [41] Then he withdrew from them about a stone's throw, knelt down, and prayed, [42] "Father, if you are willing, remove this cup from me; yet, not my will but yours be done." [43] Then an angel from heaven appeared to him and gave him strength. [44] In his anguish he prayed more earnestly, and his sweat became like great drops of blood falling down on the ground. [45] When he got up from prayer, he came to the disciples and found them sleeping because of grief, [46] and he said to them, "Why are you sleeping? Get up and pray that you may not come into the time of trial."

The Arrest

[47] While he was still speaking, suddenly a crowd came, and the one called Judas, one of the twelve, was leading them. He approached Jesus to kiss him; [48] but Jesus said to him, "Judas, is it

with a kiss that you are betraying the Son of Man?" [49] When those who were around him saw what was coming, they asked, "Lord, should we strike with the sword?" [50] Then one of them struck the slave of the high priest and cut off his right ear. [51] But Jesus said, "No more of this!" And he touched his ear and healed him. [52] Then Jesus said to the chief priests, the officers of the temple police, and the elders who had come for him, "Have you come out with swords and clubs as if I were a bandit? [53] When I was with you day after day in the temple, you did not lay hands on me. But this is your hour, and the power of darkness!"

Jesus in the Hands of the Guards, Peter's Denial

[54] Then they seized him and led him away, bringing him into the high priest's house. But Peter was following at a distance. [55] When they had kindled a fire in the middle of the courtyard and sat down together, Peter sat among them.

[56] Then a servant-girl, seeing him in the firelight, stared at him and said, "This man also was with him." [57] But he denied it, saying, "Woman, I do not know him." [58] A little later someone else, on seeing him, said, "You also are one of them." But Peter said, "Man, I am not!" [59] Then about an hour later still another kept insisting, "Surely this man also was with him; for he is a Galilean." [60] But Peter said, "Man, I do not know what you are talking about!" At that moment, while he was still speaking, the cock crowed. [61] The Lord turned and looked at Peter. Then Peter remembered the word of the Lord, how he had said to him, "Before the cock crows today, you will deny me three times." [62] And he went out and wept bitterly.

[63] Now the men who were holding Jesus began to mock him and beat him; [64] they also blindfolded him and kept asking him, "Prophesy! Who is it that struck you?" [65] They kept heaping many other insults on him.

Jesus Before the Sanhedrin

[66] When day came, the assembly of the elders of the people, both chief priests and scribes, gathered together, and they brought him to their council. [67] They said, "If you are the Messiah, tell us." He

replied, "If I tell you, you will not believe; [68] and if I question you, you will not answer. [69] But from now on the Son of Man will be seated at the right hand of the power of God." [70] All of them asked, "Are you, then, the Son of God?" He said to them, "You say that I am." [71] Then they said, "What further testimony do we need? We have heard it ourselves from his own lips!"

Jesus Before Pilate

23   Then the assembly rose as a body and brought Jesus before Pilate. [2] They began to accuse him, saying, "We found this man perverting our nation, forbidding us to pay taxes to the emperor, and saying that he himself is the Messiah, a king." [3] Then Pilate asked him, "Are you the king of the Jews?" He answered, "You say so." [4] Then Pilate said to the chief priests and the crowds, "I find no basis for an accusation against this man." [5] But they were insistent and said, "He stirs up the people by teaching throughout all Judea, from Galilee where he began even to this place."

Jesus Before Herod

[6] When Pilate heard this, he asked whether the man was a Galilean. [7] And when he learned that he was under Herod's jurisdiction, he sent him off to Herod, who was himself in Jerusalem at that time. [8] When Herod saw Jesus, he was very glad, for he had been wanting to see him for a long time, because he had heard about him and was hoping to see him perform some sign. [9] He questioned him at some length, but Jesus gave him no answer. [10] The chief priests and the scribes stood by, vehemently accusing him. [11] Even Herod with his soldiers treated him with contempt and mocked him; then he put an elegant robe on him, and sent him back to Pilate. [12] That same day Herod and Pilate became friends with each other; before this they had been enemies.

Jesus' Condemnation

[13] Pilate then called together the chief priests, the leaders, and the people, [14] and said to them, "You brought me this man as one who was perverting the people; and here I have examined him in your presence and have not found this man guilty of any of your

charges against him. [15] Neither has Herod, for he sent him back to us. Indeed, he has done nothing to deserve death. [16] I will therefore have him flogged and release him."*

[18] Then they all shouted out together, "Away with this fellow! Release Barabbas for us!" [19] (This was a man who had been put in prison for an insurrection that had taken place in the city, and for murder.) [20] Pilate, wanting to release Jesus, addressed them again; [21] but they kept shouting, "Crucify, crucify him!" [22] A third time he said to them, "Why, what evil has he done? I have found in him no ground for the sentence of death; I will therefore have him flogged and then release him." [23] But they kept urgently demanding with loud shouts that he should be crucified; and their voices prevailed. [24] So Pilate gave his verdict that their demand should be granted. [25] He released the man they asked for, the one who had been put in prison for insurrection and murder, and he handed Jesus over as they wished.

The Way to Calvary

[26] As they led him away, they seized a man, Simon of Cyrene, who was coming from the country, and they laid the cross on him, and made him carry it behind Jesus. [27] A great number of the people followed him, and among them were women who were beating their breasts and wailing for him. [28] But Jesus turned to them and said, "Daughters of Jerusalem, do not weep for me, but weep for yourselves and for your children. [29] For the days are surely coming when they will say, 'Blessed are the barren, and the wombs that never bore, and the breasts that never nursed.' [30] Then they will begin to say to the mountains, 'Fall on us'; and to the hills, 'Cover us.' [31] For if they do this when the wood is green, what will happen when it is dry?" [32] Two others also, who were criminals, were led away to be put to death with him.

---

* Verse 17, in current numeration, probably does not relay the original text from Luke's Gospel. The basic sense of the phrase (the manuscripts that report this phrase abound in variations) runs: "Now, he was supposed to release someone to them at each feast."

Jesus Is Crucified

³³ When they came to the place that is called The Skull, they crucified Jesus there with the criminals, one on his right and one on his left. ³⁴ Then Jesus said, "Father, forgive them; for they do not know what they are doing." And they cast lots to divide his clothing. ³⁵ And the people stood by, watching; but the leaders scoffed at him, saying, "He saved others; let him save himself if he is the Messiah of God, his chosen one!" ³⁶ The soldiers also mocked him, coming up and offering him sour wine, ³⁷ and saying, "If you are the King of the Jews, save yourself!" ³⁸ There was also an inscription over him, "This is the King of the Jews."

³⁹ One of the criminals who were hanged there kept deriding him and saying, "Are you not the Messiah? Save yourself and us!" ⁴⁰ But the other rebuked him, saying, "Do you not fear God, since you are under the same sentence of condemnation? ⁴¹ And we indeed have been condemned justly, for we are getting what we deserve for our deeds, but this man has done nothing wrong." ⁴² Then he said, "Jesus, remember me when you come into your kingdom." ⁴³ He replied, "Truly I tell you, today you will be with me in Paradise."

The Death of Jesus

⁴⁴ It was now about noon, and darkness came over the whole land until three in the afternoon, ⁴⁵ while the sun's light failed; and the curtain of the temple was torn in two. ⁴⁶ Then Jesus, crying with a loud voice, said, "Father, into your hands I commend my spirit." Having said this, he breathed his last. ⁴⁷ When the centurion saw what had taken place, he praised God and said, "Certainly this man was innocent." ⁴⁸ And when all the crowds who had gathered there for this spectacle saw what had taken place, they returned home, beating their breasts. ⁴⁹ But all his acquaintances, including the women who had followed him from Galilee, stood at a distance, watching these things.

The Burial of Jesus

⁵⁰ Now there was a good and righteous man named Joseph, who, though a member of the council, ⁵¹ had not agreed to their plan

and action. He came from the Jewish town of Arimathea, and he was waiting expectantly for the kingdom of God. [52] This man went to Pilate and asked for the body of Jesus. [53] Then he took it down, wrapped it in a linen cloth, and laid it in a rock-hewn tomb where no one had ever been laid. [54] It was the day of Preparation, and the sabbath was beginning. [55] The women who had come with him from Galilee followed, and they saw the tomb and how his body was laid. [56] Then they returned, and prepared spices and ointments. On the sabbath they rested according to the commandment.

The Message Received at the Tomb

24   But on the first day of the week, at early dawn, they came to the tomb, taking the spices that they had prepared. [2] They found the stone rolled away from the tomb, [3] but when they went in, they did not find the body. [4] While they were perplexed about this, suddenly two men in dazzling clothes stood beside them. [5] The women were terrified and bowed their faces to the ground, but the men said to them, "Why do you look for the living among the dead? He is not here, but has risen. [6] Remember how he told you, while he was still in Galilee, [7] that the Son of Man must be handed over to sinners, and be crucified, and on the third day rise again." [8] Then they remembered his words, [9] and returning from the tomb, they told all this to the eleven and to all the rest. [10] Now it was Mary Magdalene, Joanna, Mary the mother of James, and the other women with them who told this to the apostles. [11] But these words seemed to them an idle tale, and they did not believe them. [12] But Peter got up and ran to the tomb; stooping and looking in, he saw the linen cloths by themselves; then he went home, amazed at what had happened.

The Appearance to the Disciples at Emmaus

[13] Now on that same day two of them were going to a village called Emmaus, about seven miles from Jerusalem, [14] and talking with each other about all these things that had happened. [15] While they were talking and discussing, Jesus himself came near and went with them, [16] but their eyes were kept from recognizing him.

¹⁷ And he said to them, "What are you discussing with each other while you walk along?" They stood still, looking sad. ¹⁸ Then one of them, whose name was Cleopas, answered him, "Are you the only stranger in Jerusalem who does not know the things that have taken place there in these days?" ¹⁹ He asked them, "What things?" They replied, "The things about Jesus of Nazareth, who was a prophet mighty in deed and word before God and all the people, ²⁰ and how our chief priests and leaders handed him over to be condemned to death and crucified him. ²¹ But we had hoped that he was the one to redeem Israel. Yes, and besides all this, it is now the third day since these things took place. ²² Moreover, some women of our group astounded us. They were at the tomb early this morning, ²³ and when they did not find his body there, they came back and told us that they had indeed seen a vision of angels who said that he was alive. ²⁴ Some of those who were with us went to the tomb and found it just as the women had said; but they did not see him."

²⁵ Then he said to them, "Oh, how foolish you are, and how slow of heart to believe all that the prophets have declared! ²⁶ Was it not necessary that the Messiah should suffer these things and then enter into his glory?" ²⁷ Then beginning with Moses and all the prophets, he interpreted to them the things about himself in all the scriptures.

²⁸ As they came near the village to which they were going, he walked ahead as if he were going on. ²⁹ But they urged him strongly, saying, "Stay with us, because it is almost evening and the day is now nearly over." So he went in to stay with them. ³⁰ When he was at the table with them, he took bread, blessed and broke it, and gave it to them. ³¹ Then their eyes were opened, and they recognized him; and he vanished from their sight. ³² They said to each other, "Were not our hearts burning within us while he was talking to us on the road, while he was opening the scriptures to us?"

³³ That same hour they got up and returned to Jerusalem; and they found the eleven and their companions gathered together. ³⁴ They were saying, "The Lord has risen indeed, and he has appeared to Simon!"

[35] Then they told what had happened on the road, and how he had been made known to them in the breaking of the bread.

The Appearance to the Eleven

[36] While they were talking about this, Jesus himself stood among them and said to them, "Peace be with you." [37] They were startled and terrified, and thought that they were seeing a ghost. [38] He said to them, "Why are you frightened, and why do doubts arise in your hearts? [39] Look at my hands and my feet; see that it is I myself. Touch me and see; for a ghost does not have flesh and bones as you see that I have." [40] And when he had said this, he showed them his hands and his feet. [41] While in their joy they were disbelieving and still wondering, he said to them, "Have you anything here to eat?" [42] They gave him a piece of broiled fish, [43] and he took it and ate in their presence.

[44] Then he said to them, "These are my words that I spoke to you while I was still with you—that everything written about me in the law of Moses, the prophets, and the psalms must be fulfilled." [45] Then he opened their minds to understand the scriptures, [46] and he said to them, "Thus it is written, that the Messiah is to suffer and to rise from the dead on the third day, [47] and that repentance and forgiveness of sins is to be proclaimed in his name to all nations, beginning from Jerusalem. [48] You are witnesses of these things. [49] And see, I am sending upon you what my Father promised; so stay here in the city until you have been clothed with power from on high."

The Ascension

[50] Then he led them out as far as Bethany, and, lifting up his hands, he blessed them. [51] While he was blessing them, he withdrew from them and was carried up into heaven. [52] And they worshiped him, and returned to Jerusalem with great joy; [53] and they were continually in the temple blessing God.

The *Gospel of Peter**

[. . .] 1   ¹ But of the Jews none washed their hands, neither Herod nor any one of his judges. And as they would not wash, Pilate arose. ² And then Herod the king commanded that the Lord should be marched off, saying to them, "What I have commanded you to do to him, do ye."

Joseph of Arimathea's Request

2   ³ Now there stood there Joseph, the friend of Pilate and of the Lord, and knowing that they were about to crucify him he came to Pilate and begged the body of the Lord for burial. ⁴And Pilate sent to Herod and begged his body. ⁵And Herod said, "Brother Pilate, even if no one had begged him, we should bury him, since the Sabbath is drawing on. For it stands written in the law: The sun should not set on one that has been put to death." And he delivered him to the people on the day before the unleavened bread, their feast.

Abuse at the Hand of the Jews

3   ⁶ So they took the Lord and pushed him in great haste and said, "Let us hale the Son of God now that we have gotten power

---

* The translation cited here, as earlier, is Christian Maurer's *New Testament Apocrypha*, vol. 1, ed. Wilhelm Schneemelcher, rev. ed. (Louisville, KY: Westminster/John Knox Press, 1991), 223–27.

over him." [7] And they put upon him a purple robe and set him on the judgment seat and said, "Judge righteously, O King of Israel!" [8] And one of them brought a crown of thorns and put it on the Lord's head. [9] And others who stood by spat on his face, and others buffeted him on the cheeks, others nudged him with a reed, and some scourged him, saying, "With such honour let us honour the Son of God."

The Crucifixion

4   [10] And they brought two malefactors and crucified the Lord in the midst between them. But he held his peace, as if he felt no pain. [11] And when they had set up the cross, they wrote upon it: This is the King of Israel. [12] And they laid down his garments before him and divided them among themselves and cast the lot upon them. [13] But one of the malefactors rebuked them, saying, "We have landed in suffering for the deeds of wickedness which we have committed, but this man, who has become the saviour of men, what wrong has he done you?" [14]And they were wroth with him and commanded that his legs should not be broken, so that he might die in torments.

5   [15] Now it was midday and a darkness covered all Judaea. And they became anxious and uneasy lest the sun had already set, since he was still alive. [For] it stands written for them: the sun should not set on one that has been put to death. [16] And one of them said, "Give him to drink gall with vinegar." And they mixed it and gave him to drink. [17] And they fulfilled all things and completed the measure of their sins on their head. [18] And many went about with lamps, since they supposed that it was night, [and] they stumbled. [19] And the Lord called out and cried, "My power, O power, thou hast forsaken me!" And having said this he was taken up. [20] And at the same hour the veil of the temple in Jerusalem was rent in two.

The Deposition from the Cross and the Burial of the Lord's Body

6   [21] And then the Jews drew the nails from the hands of the Lord and laid him on the earth. And the whole earth shook and there came a great fear. [22] Then the sun shone [again], and it was found

to be the ninth hour. [23] And the Jews rejoiced and gave his body to Joseph that he might bury it, since he had seen all the good that he [= Jesus] had done. [24] And he took the Lord, washed him, wrapped him in linen and brought him into his own sepulchre, called Joseph's Garden.

The Reaction of the Jews and the Disciples

7   [25] Then the Jews and the elders and the priests, perceiving what great evil they had done to themselves, began to lament and to say, "Woe on our sins, the judgment and the end of Jerusalem is drawn nigh." [26] But I mourned with my fellows, and being wounded in heart we hid ourselves, for we were sought after by them as evildoers and as persons who wanted to set fire to the Temple. [27] Because of all these things we were fasting and sat mourning and weeping night and day until the sabbath.

The Guards at the Tomb

8   [28] But the scribes and pharisees and elders, being assembled together and hearing that all the people were murmuring and beating their breasts, saying, "If at his death these exceeding great signs have come to pass, behold how righteous he was!"— [29] were afraid and came to Pilate, entreating him and saying, [30] "Give us soldiers that we may watch his sepulchre for three days, lest his disciples come and steal him away and the people suppose that he is risen from the dead, and do us harm." [31] And Pilate gave them Petronius the centurion with soldiers to watch the sepulchre. And with them there came elders and scribes to the sepulchre. [32] And all who were there, together with the centurion and the soldiers, rolled thither a great stone and laid it against the entrance to the sepulchre [33] and put on it seven seals, pitched a tent and kept watch.

9   [34] Early in the morning, when the sabbath dawned, there came a crowd from Jerusalem and the country round about to see the sepulchre that had been sealed.

The Guards' Visions

[35] Now in the night in which the Lord's day dawned, when the soldiers, two by two in every watch, were keeping guard, there rang

out a loud voice in heaven, [36] and they saw the heavens opened and two men come down from there in a great brightness and draw nigh to the sepulchre. [37] That stone which had been laid against the entrance to the sepulchre started of itself to roll and gave way to the side, and the sepulchre was opened, and both the young men entered in.

10   [38] When now those soldiers saw this, they awakened the centurion and the elders—for they also were there to assist at the watch. [39] And whilst they were relating what they had seen, they saw again three men come out from the sepulchre, and two of them sustaining the other, and a cross following them, [40] and the heads of the two reaching to heaven, but that of him who was led of them by the hand overpassing the heavens. [41] And they heard a voice out of the heavens crying, "Hast thou preached to them that sleep?" [42] and from the cross there was heard the answer, "Yea."

11   [43] Those men therefore took counsel with one another to go and report this to Pilate. [44] And whilst they were still deliberating, the heavens were again seen to open, and a man descended and entered into the sepulchre.

The Guards Before Pilate

[45] When those who were of the centurion's company saw this, they hastened by night to Pilate, abandoning the sepulchre which they were guarding, and reported everything that they had seen, being full of disquietude and saying, "In truth he was the Son of God." [46] Pilate answered and said, "I am clean from the blood of the Son of God, upon such a thing have you decided." [47] Then all came to him, beseeching him and urgently calling upon him to command the centurion and the soldiers to tell no one what they had seen. [48] "For it is better for us," they said, "to make ourselves guilty of the greatest sin before God than to fall into the hands of the people of the Jews and be stoned." [49] Pilate therefore commanded the centurion and the soldiers to say nothing.

The Women at the Tomb

12   [50] Early in the morning of the Lord's day Mary Magdalene, a woman disciple of the Lord—for fear of the Jews, since [they]

were inflamed with wrath, she had not done at the sepulchre of the Lord what women are wont to do for those beloved of them who die—took [51] with her her women friends and came to the sepulchre where he was laid. [52] And they feared lest the Jews should see them, and said, "Although we could not weep and lament on that day when he was crucified, yet let us now do so at his sepulchre. [53] But who will roll away for us the stone also that is set on the entrance to the sepulchre, that we may go in and sit beside him and do what is due?— [54] For the stone was great—and we fear lest any one see us. And if we cannot do so, let us at least put down at the entrance what we bring for a memorial of him and let us weep and lament until we have again gone home."

13   [55] So they went and found the sepulchre opened. And they came near, stooped down, and saw there a young man sitting in the midst of the sepulchre, comely and clothed with a brightly shining robe, who said to them, [56] "Wherefore are ye come? Whom seek ye? Not him that was crucified? He is risen and gone. But if ye believe not, stoop this way and see the place where he lay, for he is not here. For he is risen and is gone thither whence he was sent.' [57] Then the woman fled affrighted.

Beginning of the Appearance of the Lord to Peter, Andrew, Levi . . .
14   [58] Now it was the last day of unleavened bread and many went away and repaired to their homes, since the feast was at an end. [59] But we, the twelve disciples of the Lord, wept and mourned, and each one, very grieved for what had come to pass, went to his own home. [60] But I, Simon Peter, and my brother Andrew took our nets and went to the sea. And there was with us Levi, the son of Alphaeus, whom the Lord . . .

Chronological Bibliography

Wlassak, Moriz. "Zum römischen Provinzialprozess." In *Sitzungsberichte der Akademie der Wissenschaften in Wien, Philosophisch-historische Klasse* 190 Bd. 4. Vienna: A. Hölder, 1919.

Bertram, Georg. *Die Leidensgeschichte Jesu und der Christuskult. Eine formgeschichtliche Untersuchung.* Göttingen: Vandenhoeck & Ruprecht, 1922.

Lietzmann, Hans. "Der Prozess Jesu." In *Sitzungsberichte der Preussischen Akademie der Wissenschaften, Philosophisch-historische Klasse* 1931, 14:313–22. Berlin: Akademie der Wissenschaften, 1934. Reprint, in *Kleine Schriften* 2:251–63. Berlin: Akademie-Verlag, 1958.

Finegan, Jack. *Die Überlieferung der Leidens- und Auferstehungsgeschichte Jesu.* Giessen: A. Töpelmann, 1934.

Bickermann, Elias. "Utilitas Crucis. Observations sur les récits du procès de Jésus dans les évangiles canoniques." *Revue de l'histoire des religions* 112 (1935): 169–241.

Surkau, Hans Werner. *Martyrien in jüdischer und frühchristlicher Zeit.* Göttingen: Vandenhoeck & Ruprecht, 1938.

Visscher, Fernand de. *Les édits d'Auguste découverts à Cyrène.* Louvain: Bureau du Recueil, Bibliothèque de l'Université, 1940. Reprint, Osnabrück: O. Zeller, 1965.

Taylor, Vincent. *Jesus and His Sacrifice: A Study of the Passion-Sayings in the Gospels.* London: Macmillan, 1943.

Moreau, Jacques. *Les plus anciens témoignages profanes sur Jésus.* Brussels: Office de publicité, 1944.

Schelkle, Karl Hermann. *Die Passion Jesu in der Verkündigung des Neuen Testaments. Ein Beitrag zur Formgeschichte und zur Theologie des Neuen Testaments.* Heidelberg: F. H. Kerle, 1948.

Pflaum, Hans-Georg. *Essai sur les procurateurs équestres sous le Haut-Empire romain.* Paris: A. Maisonneuve, 1950.

Kilpatrick, George Dunbar. *The Trial of Jesus.* London: Oxford University Press, 1953.

Dahl, Nils Alstrup. "Die Passionsgeschichte bei Matthäus.' *New Testament Studies* 2 (1955): 17-32.

Parrot, André. *Golgotha et Saint-Sépulcre*. Neuchâtel: Delachaux et Niestlé, 1955.

Knox, John. *The Death of Christ: The Cross in New Testament History and Faith*. New York: Abingdon Press, 1958.

Pflaum, Hans-Georg. *Les carrières procuratoriennes équestres sous le Haut-Empire romain*. 4 vols. Paris: P. Geuthner, 1960–61.

Linton, Olof. "The Trial of Jesus and the Interpretation of Psalm 110." *New Testament Studies* 7 (1961): 258–62.

Oyen, Hendrik van. "Neue Forschungen über den Prozess Jesu." *Christlich-jüdisches Forum. Mitteilungsblatt der christlich-jüdischen Arbeitsgemeinschaft in der Schweiz* 26 (1961): 1–3.

Winter, Paul. *On the Trial of Jesus*. Berlin: de Gruyter, 1961.

Bleicken, Jochen. *Senatsgericht und Kaisergericht. Eine Studie zur Entwicklung des Prozessrechtes im frühen Prinzipat*. Abhandlungen der Akademie der Wissenschaften in Göttingen, Philologisch-historische Klasse 3 Folge 53. Göttingen: Vandenhoeck & Ruprecht, 1962.

Vardaman, Jerry. "A New Inscription Which Mentions Pilate as Prefect." *Journal of Biblical Literature* 81 (1962): 70–71.

Sherwin-White, A. N. *Roman Society and Roman Law in the New Testament*. Oxford: Clarendon Press, 1963.

Camacho-Evangelista, F. "La epistula di Claudio Quartino y el proceso en contumacia en las provincias (provincia Tarraconense)." *Revue internationale des droits de l'antiquité*, 3rd ser., 11 (1964): 299–319.

Finegan, Jack. *Handbook of Biblical Chronology: Principles of Time Reckoning in the Ancient World and Problems of Chronology in the Bible*. Princeton, NJ: Princeton University Press, 1964.

Gaudemet, Jean. "La juridiction provinciale d'après la correspondance entre Pline et Trajan." *Revue internationale des droits de l'antiquité*, 3rd ser., 11 (1964): 335–53.

Lohse, Eduard. *Die Geschichte des Leidens und Sterbens Jesu Christi*. Gütersloh: G. Mohn, 1964.

Luzzatto, G. L. "In tema di processo provinciale e autonomia cittadina." *Revue internationale des droits de l'antiquité*, 3rd ser., 11 (1964): 355–62.

Visscher, Fernand de. "La justice romaine en Cyrénaïque." *Revue internationale des droits de l'antiquité*, 3rd ser., 11 (1964): 321–33.

Colin, Jean. *Les villes libres de l'Orient gréco-romain et l'envoi au supplice par acclamations populaires*. Brussels: Latomus, 1965.

Jaubert, Annie. *The Date of the Last Supper*. Staten Island, NY: Alba House, 1965.

Benoit, Pierre. *Passion et résurrection du Seigneur*. Paris: Cerf, 1966.

D'Ors, Alvaro. "Epigrafia juridica griega y romana (VIII)." *Studia et Documenta Historiae et Juris* 32 (1966): 472; and "(IX)"; Ibid. 35 (1969): 522 (bibliography).

Jepsen, Alfred and August Strobel. "Zeitrechnung" in *Biblisch-historisches Handwörterbuch*, edited by Bo Reicke and Leonhard Rost, vol. 3, cols. 2211–28.

Göttingen: Vandenhoeck & Ruprecht, 1966.

Brandon, S. G. F. *Jesus and the Zealots: A Study of the Political Factor in Primitive Christianity.* Manchester: Manchester University Press, 1967.

Conzelmann, Hans. *Zur Bedeutung des Todes Jesu. Exegetische Beiträge.* Gütersloh: Gütersloher Verlagshaus, 1967.

Gaudemet, Jean. *Institutions de l'Antiquité.* Paris: Sirey, 1967.

Vanhoye, Albert. "Structure et théologie des récits de la Passion dans les Évangiles synoptiques." *Nouvelle Revue Théologique* 99 (1967): 135–63.

Brandon, S. G. F. *The Trial of Jesus of Nazareth.* New York: Stein and Day, 1968.

Francisci, Pietro de. "Brevi Riflessioni intorno al 'processo' di Gesù." In *Studi in onore di Giuseppe Grosso,* 3–25. Torino: G. Giappichelli, 1968.

Longo, G. "Il Processo di Gesù." In *Studi in onore di Giuseppe Grosso,* 529–605. Torino: G. Giappichelli, 1968.

Volkmann, Hans. "Die Pilatus Inschrift von Caesarea Maritima." *Gymnasium* 75 (1968): 124–35.

Blinzler, Josef. *Der Prozess Jesu. Das jüdische und das römische Gerichtsverfahren gegen Jesus Christus auf Grund der ältesten Zeugnisse dargestellt und beurteilt.* Regensburg: F. Pustet, 1969.

Schneider, Gerhard. *Verleugnung, Verspottung und Verhör Jesu nach Lukas 22, 54–71. Studien zur lukanischen Darstellung der Passion.* Munich: Kösel, 1969.

Vidal Pazos, Raimundo. *Jurídicas reflexiones en torno al proceso de Cristo.* La Coruña: Academia Gallega de Jurisprudencia y Legislación, 1969.

Wilson, Robert McL. "The New Passion of Jesus in the Light of the New Testament and Apocrypha." In *Neotestamentica et Semitica: Studies in Honour of Matthew Black,* edited by E. Earle Ellis and Max Wilcox, 264–71. Edinburgh: T. & T. Clark, 1969.

Bammel, Ernst, ed. *The Trial of Jesus: Cambridge Studies in Honour of C. F. D. Moule.* London: SCM Press, 1970.

Burkill, T. Alec. "Condemnation of Jesus: A Critique of Sherwin-White's Thesis." *Novum Testamentum* 12 (1970): 321–42.

Cullman, Oscar. *Jésus et les révolutionnaires de son temps. Culte, société, politique.* Neuchâtel: Delachaux et Niestlé, 1970.

Gnilka, Joachim. "Die Verhandlungen vor dem Synhedrion und vor Pilatus nach Markus 14,53–15,5." In *Evangelisch-Katholischer Kommentar zum Neuen Testament, Vorarbeiten Heft 2,* 5–21. Neukirchen: Neukirchener Verlag, 1970.

Grass, Hans. *Ostergeschehen und Osterberichte.* 4th ed. Göttingen: Vandenhoeck & Ruprecht, 1970.

Haas, Nicu. "Anthropological Observations on the Skeletal Remains from Giv'at ha-Mivtar." *Israel Exploration Journal* 20 (1970): 38–59.

Hahn, Ferdinand. "Der Prozess Jesu nach dem Johannesevangelium. Eine redaktionsgeschichte Untersuchung." In *Evangelisch-Katholischer Kommentar zum Neuen Testament, Vorarbeiten Heft 2,* 23–96. Neukirchen: Neukirchener Verlag, 1970.

Linnemann, Eta. *Studien zur Passionsgeschichte*. Göttingen: Vandenhoeck & Ruprecht, 1970.

Lohse, Eduard. Review of *The Trial of Jesus of Nazareth*, by S. G. F. Brandon. *Novum Testamentum* 12 (1970): 78–79.

Naveh, Joseph. "The Ossuary Inscriptions from Giv'at ha-Mivtar." *Israel Exploration Journal* 20 (1970): 33–37.

Tzaferis, Vassilios. "Jewish Tombs at and near Giv'at ha-Mivtar, Jerusalem." *Israel Exploration Journal* 20 (1970): 18–32.

Wilson, William Riley. *The Execution of Jesus: A Judicial, Literary, and Historical Investigation*. New York: Scribner, 1970.

Briend, Jacques. "La sépulture d'un crucifié." *Bible et Terre Sainte* 133 (1971): 6–10.

Catchpole, David R. *The Trial of Jesus: A Study in the Gospels and Jewish Historiography from 1770 to the Present Day*. Leiden: E. J. Brill, 1971.

Cohn, Haim Hermann. *The Trial and Death of Jesus*. New York: Harper & Row, 1971.

Crespy, Georges. "La signification politique de la mort du Christ." *Lumière et Vie* 101 (1971): 89–109.

Gordis, Robert, ed. "Trial of Jesus in the Light of History: A Symposium." *Judaism* 20 (1971): 6–74.

Pines, Shlomo. *An Arabic Version of the Testimonium Flavianum and Its Implications*. Jerusalem: Israel Academy of Sciences and Humanities, 1971.

Dauer, Anton. *Die Passionsgeschichte im Johannesevangelium. Eine traditionsgeschichtliche und theologische Untersuchung zu Joh. 18, 1–19, 30*. Studien zum Alten und Neuen Testaments 30. Munich: Kösel-Verlag, 1972.

Gorman, Ralph. *The Trial of Christ: A Reappraisal*. Huntington, IN: Our Sunday Visitor, 1972.

Horbury, William. "Passion Narratives and Historical Criticism." *Theology* 75 (1972): 58–71.

Taylor, Vincent. *The Passion Narrative of St. Luke: A Critical and Historical Investigation*. Cambridge: Cambridge University Press, 1972.

Weber, Hans Ruedi. "Freedom Fighter or Prince of Peace." *Encounter* 8 (1972): 1–24.

Fuchs, E. "L'évangile de Jésus." *Les Cahiers Protestants* 1–2 (1973): 67–80.

Hengel, Martin. *Jésus et la violence révolutionnaire*. Translated by Christoph von Schönborn. Paris: Cerf, 1973.

Schneider, Gerhard. *Die Passion Jesus nach den drei älteren Evangelien*. Munich: Kösel, 1973.

Sloyan, Gerard. *Jesus on Trial: The Development of the Passion Narratives and Their Historical and Ecumenical Implications*. Philadelphia: Fortress Press, 1973.

Dhanis, Édouard, ed. *Resurrexit. Actes du Symposium international sur la résurrection de Jésus, Rome, 1970*. Rome: Libreria editrice vaticana, 1974.

Alsup, John E. *The Post-Resurrection Appearance Stories of the Gospel Tradition: A History-of-Tradition Analysis*. Stuttgart: Calwer-Verlag, 1975.

Hengel, Martin. *Crucifixion in the Ancient World and the Folly of the Message of the Cross*. Translated by John Bowden. London: SCM Press, 1977.

Bacchiocchi, Samuele. *The Time of the Crucifixion and the Resurrection with Other Essays*. Biblical Perspectives 4. Berrien Springs, MI: Biblical Perspectives, 1985.

Fricke, Weddig. *Standrechtlich gekreuzigt. Person und Prozess des Jesus aus Galiläa*. Frankfurt: Mai Verlag, 1986.

Thomas, Gordon. *The Trial: The Life and Inevitable Crucifixion of Jesus*. London: Bantam Press, 1987.

Crossan, John Dominic. *The Cross That Spoke: The Origins of the Passion Narrative*. San Francisco: Harper & Row, 1988.

Pesch, Rudolf. *Der Prozess Jesu geht weiter*. Herderbücherei 1507. Freiburg: Herder Taschenbuch Verlag, 1988.

Bauer, Rick. *The Anatomy of Calvary: An In-Depth Study of the Cross*. Joplin, MO: College Press, 1989.

Foreman, Dale M. *Crucify Him: A Lawyer Looks at the Trial of Jesus*. Grand Rapids: Zondervan, 1990.

Crossan, John Dominic. *The Historical Jesus: The Life of a Mediterranean Jewish Peasant*. San Francisco: Harper Collins, 1991.

McLaren, James S. *Power and Politics in Palestine: The Jews and the Governing of Their Land, 100 BC–AD 70*. Journal for the Study of the New Testament: Supplement Series 63. Sheffield: JSOT Press, 1991.

Brown, Raymond E. *The Death of the Messiah, from Gethsemane to the Grave: A Commentary on the Passion Narratives in the Four Gospels*. New York: Doubleday, 1994.

Légasse, Simon. *Le procès de Jésus, l'histoire*. Paris: Cerf, 1994.

Carroll, John T., and Joel B. Green, with Robert E. Van Voorst, Joel Marcus, and Donald Senior. *The Death of Jesus in Early Christianity*. Peabody, MA: Hendrickson, 1995.

Crossan, John Dominic. *Who Killed Jesus? Exposing the Roots of Anti-Semitism in the Gospel Story of the Death of Jesus*. San Francisco: HarperSanFrancisco, 1995.

Fricke, Weddig. *Der Fall Jesus. Eine juristische Beweisführung*. Hamburg: Rasch und Röhring Verlag, 1995.

Lüdemann, Gerd. *What Really Happened to Jesus: A Historical Approach to the Resurrection*. Translated by John Bowden. Louisville, KY: Westminster John Knox Press, 1995.

Sloyan, Gerard. *The Crucifixion of Jesus: History, Myth, Faith*. Minneapolis: Fortress Press, 1995.

Watson, Alan. *The Trial of Jesus*. Athens, GA: University of Georgia Press, 1995.

Boer, Martinus C. de. *Johannine Perspectives on the Death of Jesus*. Kampen: Pharos, 1996.

Bovon, François. *L'Évangile selon saint Luc (9,51–14,35)*. Commentaire du Nouveau Testament 3b. Geneva: Labor et Fides, 1996.

Egger, Peter. *"Crucifixus sub Pontio Pilato". Das "crimen" Jesu von Nazareth im Spannungsfeld römischer und jüdischer Verwaltungs- und Rechtsstrukturen.* Neutestamentliche Abhandlungen, NF 32. Münster: Aschendorff, 1997.

Gounelle, Rémi, and Zbigniew Izydorczyk. *L'Évangile de Nicodème.* Apocryphes 9. Turnhout: Brepols, 1997.

Rivkin, Ellis. *What Crucified Jesus? Messianism, Pharisaism, and the Development of Christianity.* New York: UAHC Press, 1997.

Amarelli, Francesco, and Francesco Lucrezi. *Il processo contro Gesù.* Quaestiones 2. Naples: Jovene, 1999.

Boyarin, Daniel. *Dying for God: Martyrdom and the Making of Christianity and Judaism.* Stanford, CA: Stanford University Press, 1999.

Ewen, Pamela Binnings. *Faith on Trial.* Nashville, TN: Broadman & Holman, 1999.

Patella, Michael. *The Death of Jesus: The Diabolical Force and the Ministering Angel; Luke 23.44–49.* Paris: J. Gabalda, 1999.

Heusler, Erika. *Kapitalprozesse im lukanischen Doppelwerk. Die Verfahren gegen Jesus und Paulus in exegetischer und rechtshistorischer Analyse.* Neutestamentliche Abhandlungen, NF 38. Münster: Aschendorff, 2000.

Kollmann, Hanjo-Christoph. *Die Kreuzigung Jesu nach Joh 19, 16–22. Ein Beitrag zur Kreuzestheologie des Johannes im Vergleich mit den Synoptikern.* New York: P. Lang, 2000.

Mainville, Odette, and Daniel Marguerat. *Résurrection. L'après-mort dans le monde ancien et le Nouveau Testament.* Geneva: Labor et Fides, 2001.

Paget, Carleton. "Some Observations on Josephus and Christianity." *Journal of Theological Studies* 52 (2001): 539–624.

Neagoe, Alexandru. *The Trial of the Gospel: An Apologetic Reading of Luke's Trial Narratives.* Society for New Testament Studies Monograph Series 116. New York: Cambridge University Press, 2002.

Nodet, Étienne. *Le fils de Dieu. Procès de Jésus et évangiles.* Paris: Cerf, 2002.

Bovon, François. "The Lucan Story of the Passion of Jesus." In *Studies in Early Christianity,* 74–105. Tübingen: Mohr Siebeck, 2003.

Holzapfel, Richard Neitzel, and Thomas Wayment, eds. *From the Last Supper through the Resurrection: The Savior's Final Hours.* Salt Lake City, UT: Deseret Books, 2003.

Meinhardt, Molly Dewsnap, ed. *Jesus, the Last Day: A Collection of Essays Published by the Biblical Archaeology Society.* Washington, DC: Biblical Archaeology Society, 2003.

Puig i Tàrrech, Armand. Review of *Le fils de Dieu: Procès de Jésus et évangiles,* by Étienne Nodet. *Biblica* 84 (2003): 440–44.

Whealey, Alice. *Josephus on Jesus: The Testimonium Flavianum Controversy from Late Antiquity to Modern Times.* Studies in Biblical Literature 36. Bern: Peter Lang, 2003.

Aitken, Ellen. *Jesus' Death in Early Christian Memory: The Poetics of the Passion.* Göttingen: Vandenhoeck & Ruprecht, 2004.

Blum, Matthias. *Denn sie wissen nicht, was sie tun. Zur Rezeption der Fürbitte Jesu am Kreuz (Lk 23,34a) in der antiken jüdisch-christlichen Kontroverse.* Neutestamentliche Abhandlungen, NF 46. Münster: Aschendorff, 2004.

Boyarin, Daniel. *Border Lines: The Partition of Judaeo-Christianity.* Philadelphia: University of Pennsylvania Press, 2004.

Corley, Kathleen E., and Robert L. Webb, eds. *Jesus and Mel Gibson's* The Passion of the Christ: *The Film, the Gospels and the Claims of History.* New York: Continuum, 2004.

Gibson, Mel, et al. *The Passion of the Christ.* Beverly Hills, CA: 20th Century Fox Home Entertainment, 2004.

Kesich, Veselin. *The Passion of Christ.* Crestwood, NY: St. Vladimir's Seminary Press, 2004.

Lüdemann, Gerd. *The Resurrection of Christ: A Historical Inquiry.* Amherst, NY: Prometheus Books, 2004.

Patterson, Stephen J. *Beyond the Passion: Rethinking the Death and Life of Jesus.* Minneapolis: Fortress Press, 2004.

Tomson, Peter J. *Presumed Guilty: How the Jews Were Blamed for the Death of Jesus.* Translated by Janet Dyk. Minneapolis: Fortress Press, 2005.

Index of Ancient Sources

Index of Modern Authors

Index of Subjects

Lightning Source UK Ltd.
Milton Keynes UK
UKOW041802250413

209778UK00001B/58/P